THE SPIRITUAL EXERCISES

A Literal Translation
and
a Contemporary Reading

This book is No. 7 in
Series IV: Study Aids on Jesuit Topics

David L. Fleming, S.J.

THE SPIRITUAL EXERCISES

of St. Ignatius

A LITERAL TRANSLATION

and

A CONTEMPORARY READING

THE INSTITUTE OF JESUIT SOURCES
St. Louis, 1978

IMPRIMI POTEST: Very Reverend Leo F. Weber, S.J.
Provincial of the Missouri Province
January 19, 1978

IMPRIMATUR: Most Reverend John N. Wurm, S.T.D.,
Ph.D. Chancellor, Archdiocese of St.
Louis March 31, 1978

Second printing, 1980, with
revisions on pages 23 and 202.

© 1978 The Institute of Jesuit Sources
Fusz Memorial, St. Louis University
3700 West Pine Boulevard
St. Louis, Missouri 63108

Printed in the United States of America
Library of Congress Card Catalogue Number: 77-93429
ISBN   0-912422-28-9 paperback
         0-912422-31-9 Smyth sewn paperback
         0-912422-32-7 cloth bound

CONTENTS
A Bird's-Eye View

CONTENTS IN DETAIL FOR THE PARALLEL TEXTS

THE LITERAL TRANSLATION
of
Elder Mullan, S.J.

presented below on left-hand pages
(with a few exceptions
obvious where they occur)

CONTENTS IN DETAIL FOR THE PARALLEL TEXTS

A CONTEMPORARY READING
of
David L. Fleming, S.J.

presented below on right-hand pages
(with a few exceptions
obvious where they occur)

EDITOR'S FOREWORD

The book presented here is Father David L. Fleming's revision of his previous Experimental Edition entitled: *A Contemporary Reading of the Spiritual Exercises: A Companion to St. Ignatius' Text,* published in 1976. Since then he has profited from many suggestions made by retreatants and directors who used the earlier edition, and also from his own experience with it. Furthermore, he has added his "readings" of Ignatius' Three Methods of Prayer, Rules for Distributing Alms, Notes on Scruples, and the directives commonly termed "Rules for Thinking with the Church."

The chief addition, however, is the printing of Ignatius' own text of the *Exercises,* on pages opposite the corresponding contemporary readings. Father Fleming intended his earlier edition to be a gateway to Ignatius'· classic but difficult text, not a substitute for it. In the present volume he has made his original purpose more clearly evident and also facilitated its achievement by his readers.

St. Ignatius' book of *Spiritual Exercises* sprang from the rich mystical experiences and the dynamic spiritual principles with which God gifted him. But he was not a good stylist, and often his expression is inadequate to the vision which was clear in his own mind. He does not make facile reading. His sentences are frequently complicated or rugged, and he uses words with meanings of his own, sometimes rather technical. To make his thought more readily and pleasantly grasped by present-day readers, many translators, like those of the Bible, sometimes resort to phrases and sentences which can perhaps be called paraphrases more than precise translations—pretty much like the sentences in the Jerusalem Bible or the New American Bible as contrasted with those in the more closely literal rendering found in the Revised Standard Version. These translators of the *Exercises* who choose rather free-flowing modern phraseology are indeed acting wisely for their purposes. But present, too, is a danger: the risk that important meanings, implications, and nuances which are key principles in Ignatius' spiritual outlook will be missed, or perceived only obscurely, or in time lost from view. Hence, as is the case also with Scripture, much benefit can be gained from at least an occasional return to the primary source, Ignatius' own terminology, flavor, and strong even if difficult style.

Each kind of translation, the free and the literal, has its own advantages and disadvantages. For grasping quickly the general drift of the thought, the free translation or paraphrase is often better. For precise thinking and sharp concepts, the literal translation seems indispensable. The best procedure to gain the advantages of each and to suffer least from the disadvantages is to use them both, the freer version on some occasions and the literal on others.

Not surprisingly, therefore, the English translation chosen as best suited to the purposes of the present book is a literal version, that made from the Spanish "autograph" text of Ignatius in 1909, and published in 1914, by a member of the Jesuit Province of Maryland-New York, Elder Mullan (1865-1925). One reason for its choice was its availability. Still more important, however, is its accuracy in reproducing Ignatius' thought, nuances, and style.

Vatican Council II recommended profound study of the primitive inspiration of founders of religious institutes (Religious Life, no. 2). Father Mullan's version is a helpful means to such study of Ignatius' inspiration, and Father Fleming's contemporary readings of Ignatius' text are an aid toward the adaptation and application of that spirit to modern times. The Institute of Jesuit Sources is happy to make both these works more widely available.

George E. Ganss, S.J.
Director and General Editor
The Institute of Jesuit Sources
Epiphany, January 8, 1978

AUTHOR'S PREFACE

The present small book is intended to be a gateway to St. Ignatius' *Spiritual Exercises,* a means to make his widely renowned but difficult text more easily and quickly understood by contemporary men and women—especially by those using it for the first time in directed retreats.

The *Spiritual Exercises* of the founder of the Jesuits has been a classic retreat manual in the tradition of the Church for the past four hundred years. Spiritual classics, of their very nature, are not meant to be rewritten or tampered with.

Yet significant contributions to the understanding of the *Exercises* and its application in practice have been made throughout the centuries since the first publication of the book in 1548. During Ignatius' own lifetime and for the first fifty years after his death, various commentaries on the text of the *Exercises* were written which looked primarily to the actual practice in giving the Exercises and were called "Directories." After the official *Directory of the Spiritual Exercises* was promulgated by Father Claudio Aquaviva, General of the Society of Jesus, in 1599, there was something of a lull in this style of writing. But soon commentaries of different types—some more in the nature of theological explanation of the text, others still practice-oriented in terms of particular movements or devotions in the Church— were forthcoming. In our own more recent past, retreat manuals were written in which the conferences of a preached-style retreat were put into print so that they could both inspire other directors and help other retreatants. These books provided a certain understanding of the *Exercises,* and they also at times gave direction through the written word to those who made use of them for their own private retreats.

Today, the popularity of the directed retreat has led directors and retreatants back to the starkness of the original Ignatian text. But the text itself, despite a simplicity in style, presents difficulties in word expression, image patterns, terminology, and even in world view—for Ignatius' outlook on the world was a good deal more medieval than ours is. Often the director and retreatant of today spend time on technicalities of the saint's text—time which often could be better employed in the movement of the retreat itself. I believe that what might be helpful to people of our times would be an attempt to preserve the original sparseness of the Ignatian text, yet to express it in such a way that the book seems not quite so formidable for either the present-day director or the retreatant. I would hope that the director would find such a reexpression of the Ignatian text enlightening and opening into new depths of understanding. In a similar way, it is my desire to be able to provide a reading which the director would find is less forbidding in terminology and less tortuous in explanation when he wants to put the text in the hands of a retreatant. In other words, I want to present the text in such a way that it is as easily usable and understandable for people of today as Ignatius' text was for the people of his time.

This, then, is why I entitle my efforts "a contemporary reading of the *Spiritual Exercises.*" It is not a translation in the more usual sense of the word, for I am not struggling with a rendering of the Spanish or Latin versions. Even though I have at times expanded and rearranged some parts of the text, I do not want this work to be considered a commentary or a substitute for the text of Ignatius; it is, instead, a way of "reading" Ignatius' own text. I hope that it will always draw a person back to the original source which must remain the incentive and guide for the full movement of the retreat. In order to facilitate the movement between this "reading" and the original text of Ignatius, I have placed a very careful translation made from Ignatius' Spanish autograph text by Elder Mullan, S.J., in parallel pages with my own "reading." Father Mullan's translation has the merit not only of being quite accurate but also of capturing much of the flavor and characteristics of Ignatius' personal style. For example, the delicate balance between the grace of God and our own effort, which is reflected in his original Spanish, is maintained better by Mullan than by many more recent English translators.

To make it easier for the reader to locate corresponding sections in Ignatius' text and in my contemporary reading, I have used in both these texts the numbers in square brackets which have become common since 1928 in modern editions of the *Spiritual Exercises*—including the authoritative critical text presented in *Exercitia Spiritualia: Textus* (Rome: Historical Institute of the Society of Jesus, 1969).

I am grateful to many persons who have sent me helpful suggestions and criticism since the publication, in 1976, of the Experimental Edition of this work, which had the title *A Contemporary Reading of the Spiritual Exercises*. In the present revision I have tried to enable both men and women to read my paragraphs in a more easily self-identifying manner, by changing the Ignatian masculine identity to the first person singular or plural. This adaptation entails some necessary limitations, especially when a certain objectivity is called for in the third person. Nevertheless, in this way of "reading," I hope, both retreatants and directors will find an easier personal identity flow.

There are many minor changes. The most important, perhaps, is the revision of the Foundation. I hope to have captured a little more of the directness and challenge from the Ignatian text than I had in the Experimental Edition. I have also placed a more consistent stress on the preparatory prayer makeup throughout the formal periods of prayer. I have added, too, my own "reading" of the Three Methods of Prayer, the Rules for Distributing Alms, and the Rules to have the True Sentiment in the Church, in order to present in my revised "reading" a parallel to all the major divisions of Ignatius. I feel that what I share with my readers is the compilation of those ideas which many others have passed along to me—either in writings or in conversations or in the experiences of a retreat. My desire is that what I have myself received, digested, and found helpful may be found helpful and encouraging to others too, and also supportive of their own efforts toward both understanding the *Exercises* and making them come alive for the retreatant.

To enter into the mind and spirit of St. Ignatius is the desire of everyone who directs retreats according to the manner of his *Spiritual Exercises*. No one of us, of course, can do so fully. But it is necessary that the legacy which he left to the Church and to the Society of Jesus should be made to live on with all the passion and power which he gave to it. I pray that St. Ignatius will favor and guide this latest attempt to open up his Exercises for the men and women of our times.

David L. Fleming, S.J.
Pentecost 1977

THE PREFACE OF ELDER MULLAN, S.J.
to his translation of
The Spiritual Exercises
from the
Spanish Autograph

THE present translation of the Exercises of St. Ignatius has been made from the Spanish *Autograph* of St. Ignatius. The copy so designated is not indeed in the handwriting of the Saint, but has a good number of corrections made by him and is known to have been used by him in giving the Exercises.

St. Ignatius of Loyola was a man without any great pretensions to education at the time he wrote this book. His native language was not Spanish, but Basque. His lack of education and his imperfect acquaintance with pure Spanish are enough to make it clear that a refined use of any language, and more especially of the Spanish, or, in general, anything like a finished or even perfectly correct, style is not' to be expected in his work. Literary defects he removed to some extent, perhaps, as he continued to use and apply the book, but he is known never to have been fearful of such faults. His corrections found in this text are clearly made with a view to precision more than to anything else.

The *Autograph* of St. Ignatius was translated by Father General Roothaan into Latin and was reproduced by Father

xix

Rodeles in his edition of the Spanish text. But the original was not available to ordinary students. In 1908, however, Father General Wernz allowed the entire book to be phototyped, and in this way it was spread throughout the Society of Jesus in a large number of copies. It is one of these which has been chiefly employed by the present translator, who has, besides, made frequent use of the Manuscript itself.

After considerable study of the matter, it seemed best to make this translation as faithful and close a reproduction of the Spanish text as could be. To do so it was necessary at times to sacrifice the niceties of style, but it was thought that those who would use the book would easily forego the elegancies of diction if they could feel sure they were reading the very words of St. Ignatius. Any other form of translation than the one adopted could hardly be kept from being a partial expansion, illustration or development of the original, and would therefore have proved, to some extent, a commentary as well as a translation. This the translator has earnestly sought to avoid, preferring to leave the further work of commentary to another occasion or to other hands.

Another reason for aiming at absolute fidelity rather than style was the fact that the *Exercises* are mostly read, not continuously for any time, but piecemeal and meditatively. Literary finish would therefore not be much sought or cared for in the book, but accuracy is. For this a certain neglect of style seemed pardonable in the translation, if only the real meaning of the writer could be made clear. Perhaps some may even find a charm in the consequent want of finish, seeing it reproduces more completely the style of St. Ignatius.

The process of translating in this way the *Autograph* text is not as simple as it might seem. The first difficulty is to make sure of the exact meaning of St. Ignatius. This is obscured, at times, by his language being that of nearly 400 years ago and being not pure Spanish. Occasionally, in fact, the Saint makes new Spanish words from the Latin or Italian, or uses Spanish words in an Italian or Latin sense, or employs phrases not current except in the Schools, and sometimes even has recourse to words in their Latin form. To be sure, then, of the meaning, one must often go to other languages and to the terms adopted in Scholastic Philosophy or Theology. The meaning clear, the further difficulty comes of finding an exactly equivalent English word or phrase.

In accomplishing his task, the translator has made free use of other translations, especially of that of Father General Roothaan into Latin, that of Father Venturi into Italian, and that of Father Jennesseaux into French, and has had the use of the literal translation into Latin made, apparently, by St. Ignatius himself, copied in 1541, and formally approved by the Holy See in 1548.

Besides the last-mentioned Manuscript and printed books, the translator has to acknowledge, as he does very gratefully, his obligations to the Very Rev. Father Mathias Abad, Father Achilles Gerste and particularly Father Mariano Lecina, Editor of the *Ignatiana* in the MONUMENTA HISTORICA S. J., for aid in appreciating the Spanish text, to Fathers Michael Ahern, Peter Cusick, Walter Drum, Francis Kemper and Herbert Noonan for general revision of the translation, and above all to Father Aloysius Frumveller for an accurate collation of the translation with the original.

In conclusion, it is well to warn the reader that the *Spiritual Exercises* of St. Ignatius are not meant to be read cursorily, but to be pondered word for word and under the direction of a competent guide. Read straight on, it may well appear jejune and unsatisfactory; studied in the actual making of the *Exercises,* the very text itself cannot fail to yield ever new material for thought and prayer.

ELDER MULLAN, S. J.

GERMAN COLLEGE, ROME,
Feast of St. Ignatius, 1909.

GENERAL NOTE

In the reproduction of the text in English:

1. No change whatever is made in the wording. The proper corrections, however, of the two unimportant slips in quotation have been indicated in italics.

It may be remarked in passing that the text of Holy Scripture is not seldom given in the *Spiritual Exercises* in wording somewhat different from that of the Vulgate. Such divergences have not been noted in this translation. It will be remembered that, when the book was written, the Council of Trent had not yet put its seal on the Vulgate.

2. The head lines and the rubrics have been kept as they stand in the Manuscript. Where they were wanting, they have been supplied in italics.

3. Abbreviations have been filled out.

4. Wherever italics are used, the words in this character belong to the translator and not to St. Ignatius.

5. In the use of small and capital letters, and in the matter of punctuation and the division into paragraphs the practice of the copyist has usually not been followed. Various kinds of type, also, are used independently of the Manuscript.

6. As a matter of convenience, in citations from Holy Scripture, the modern method by chapter and verse is substituted for that of the Mss. chapter and letter. Besides, quotations are indicated by quotation marks in place of the parentheses of the Mss.

ELDER MULLAN, S. J.

PAPAL APPROBATION OF ST. IGNATIUS'
Spiritual Exercises in 1548

PAUL III, POPE
FOR A PERPETUAL REMEMBRANCE

The cares of the pastoral charge of the whole flock of Christ entrusted to Us and Our devotion to the glory and praise of God impel Us to embrace what helps the salvation of souls and their spiritual profit, and cause Us to hearken to those who petition Us for what can foster and nourish piety in the faithful.

So Our beloved son, Francis de Borgia, Duke of Gandia, has lately brought it to Our notice that Our beloved son Ignatius de Loyola, General of the Society of Jesus, erected by Us in Our beloved City and confirmed by Our Apostolic authority, has compiled certain instructions, or Spiritual Exercises, drawn from Holy Writ and from experience in the spiritual life, and has reduced them to an order which is excellently adapted to move piously the souls of the faithful, and that they are very useful and wholesome for the spiritual consolation and profit of the same. This the said Duke Francis has come to know by report from many places and by clear evidence at Barcelona, Valencia and Gandia.

Hence he has humbly begged Us to cause the aforesaid instructions and Spiritual Exercises to be examined, so that their fruit may be more spread, and more of the faithful may be induced to use them with greater devotion. And he has begged Us, should We find them worthy, to approve and praise them and out of Our Apostolic goodness to make other provision in the premises.

We, therefore, have caused these instructions and Exercises to be examined, and by the testimony of and report made to Us by Our beloved son John Cardinal Priest of the Title of St. Clement, Bishop of Burgos and Inquisitor, Our venerable Brother Philip, Bishop of Saluciae, and Our Vicar General in things spiritual at Rome, and Our beloved son Aegidius Foscararius, Master of Our Sacred Palace, have found that these Exercises are full of piety and holiness and that they are and will be extremely useful and salutary for the spiritual profit of the faithful.

We have, besides, as We should, due regard to the rich fruits which Ignatius and the aforesaid Society founded by him are constantly producing everywhere in the Church of God, and to the very great help which the said Exercises have proved in this.

Moved, then, by this petition, with the aforesaid authority, by these presents, and of Our certain knowledge, We approve, praise, and favor with the present writing the aforesaid instructions and Exercises and all and everything contained in them, and We earnestly exhort all and each of the faithful of both sexes everywhere to employ instructions and Exercises so pious and to be instructed by them.

[*Here follow regulations for the diffusion of the book, and then confirmatory clauses.*]

Given at St. Mark's in Rome under the seal of the Fisherman, 31 July, 1548, in the 14th year of Our Pontificate.

BLO. EL. FULGINEN.

THE SPIRITUAL EXERCISES

A Literal Translation
and
a Contemporary Reading

ANIMA CHRISTI—a Traditional Prayer

Soul of Christ, sanctify me.
Body of Christ, save me.
Blood of Christ, inebriate me.
Water from the side of Christ, wash me.
Passion of Christ, strengthen me.
O good Jesus, hear me;
Within thy wounds hide me;
Suffer me not to be separated from thee;
From the malignant enemy defend me;
In the hour of my death call me,
And bid me come to thee,
That with thy saints I may praise thee
Forever and ever. Amen.

THE PRAYER "SOUL OF CHRIST"

Jesus, may all that is you flow into me.
May your body and blood be my food and
    drink.
May your passion and death be my strength and
    life.
Jesus, with you by my side enough has been
    given.
May the shelter I seek be the shadow of your
    cross.
Let me not run from the love which you offer,
But hold me safe from the forces of evil.
On each of my dyings shed your light and your
    love.
Keep calling to me until that day comes,
When, with your saints, I may praise you for-
    ever. Amen.

THE LITERAL TRANSLATION

[1]

I H S

ANNOTATIONS

TO GIVE SOME UNDERSTANDING OF THE
SPIRITUAL EXERCISES WHICH FOLLOW,
AND TO ENABLE HIM WHO IS TO GIVE
AND HIM WHO IS TO RECEIVE THEM
TO HELP THEMSELVES

First Annotation. The first Annotation
is that by this name of Spiritual Exercises
is meant every way of examining one's conscience, of meditating, of contemplating, of
praying vocally and mentally, and of performing other spiritual actions, as will be said later.
For as strolling, walking and running are bodily
exercises, so every way of preparing and disposing the soul to rid itself of all the disordered
tendencies, and, after it is rid, to seek and find
the Divine Will as to the management of one's
life for the salvation of the soul, is called a
Spiritual Exercise.

[2]

Second Annotation.[1] The second is that
the person who gives to another the way and
order in which to meditate or contemplate,
ought to relate faithfully the events of such
Contemplation or Meditation, going over the
Points with only a short or summary development. For, if the person who is making the
Contemplation, takes the true groundwork
of the narrative, and, discussing and considering for himself, finds something which makes
the events a little clearer or brings them a
little more home to him — whether this comes
through his own reasoning, or because his
intellect is enlightened by the Divine power —
he will get more spiritual relish and fruit, than

---

[1] *The word* Annotation *does not occur in the original
after the first time. The same is true of similar cases in
the Mss.*

A CONTEMPORARY READING

SOME PRELIMINARY HELPS   [1]

(from the reading of the

***Spiritual Exercises, [1-20]*)**

The purpose of these observations is to provide some understanding of the spiritual exercises which follow and to serve as a help both for the retreatant and for the director of the retreat.

A. *For the Retreatant*

1. The phrase "Spiritual Exercises" takes in all the formal ways we have of making contact with God, such as meditation, contemplation, vocal prayer, devotions, examination of conscience, and so on. We are familiar with the great variety of physical exercises, such as walking, jogging, playing games such as tennis, handball, golf, or even the demands of yoga and isometrics. These physical exercises are good for tuning up muscles, improving circulation and breathing, and in general for the overall good health of the body. So, too, what we call Spiritual Exercises are good for increasing openness to the movement of the Spirit, for helping to bring to light the darknesses of sinfulness and sinful tendencies within ourselves, and for strengthening and supporting us in the effort to respond ever more faithfully to the love of God.

2. In the Spiritual Exercises which follow, we find ourselves   [3]
sometimes doing much thinking and reasoning things out. At

---

*The numbers enclosed within square brackets, e.g. [3], refer throughout this book to the paragraph numbers found in most modern editions of *The Spiritual Exercises* of St. Ignatius of Loyola, which was first published in 1548. These numbers were first added to his text in the edition published in Turin in 1928, in order to make references easier. In this present *Contemporary Reading* by Father Fleming, *Spiritual Exercises* in italics refers chiefly to Ignatius' book, Spiritual Exercises in roman type to the activities within a retreat.

if he who is giving the Exercises had much explained and amplified the meaning of the events. For it is not knowing much, but realising and relishing things interiorly, that contents and satisfies the soul.

[3]   **Third Annotation.** The third: As in all the following Spiritual Exercises, we use acts of the intellect in reasoning, and acts of the will in movements of the feelings: let us remark that, in the acts of the will, when we are speaking vocally or mentally with God our Lord, or with His Saints, greater reverence is required on our part than when we are using the intellect in understanding.

[4]   **Fourth Annotation.** The fourth: The following Exercises are divided into four parts:

First, the consideration and contemplation on the sins;

Second, the life of Christ our Lord up to Palm Sunday inclusively;

Third, the Passion of Christ our Lord;

Fourth, the Resurrection and Ascension, with the three Methods of Prayer.

Though four weeks, to correspond to this division, are spent in the Exercises, it is not to be understood that each Week has, of necessity, seven or eight days. For, as it happens that in the First Week some are slower to find what they seek — namely, contrition, sorrow and tears for their sins — and in the same way some are more diligent than others, and more acted on or tried by different spirits; it is necessary sometimes to shorten the Week, and at other times to lengthen it. The same is true of all the other subsequent Weeks, seeking out the things according to the subject matter. However, the Exercises will be finished in thirty days, a little more or less.

[5]   **Fifth Annotation.** The fifth: It is very helpful to him who is receiving the Exercises to enter into them with great courage and generosity towards his Creator and Lord, offering [1] Him all his will and liberty, that His

---

[1] Offering *is in St. Ignatius' handwriting, correcting* giving *or* presenting, *which is crossed out.*

other times, we experience far more the response of our hearts, with little or nothing for the head to be concerned about. It is good to remember that we are always in the context of prayer, whether meditative or affective, and so we should always try to maintain a spirit of deep reverence before God.

3. The most important quality in the person who enters into these Exercises is openness and generosity. As a retreatant, my one hope and desire is that I can really put myself at the disposal of God so that in all ways I seek only to respond to that love which first created me and now wraps me round with total care and concern.   [5]

4. Ordinarily, if we want to give ourselves over to the movement of these Exercises, it is most helpful to go apart from what usually surrounds us—both friends and family, job and recreation, and our usual places of home and work. There are many advantages which come from this separation, for example: (1) if I am so intent on responding ever better to the love of God wherever it will lead me in my life, I will find the kind of quiet in which the movement of God in my life becomes all the more apparent; (2) my mind will not find itself divided over many cares, but rather its one concern will be to follow the lead of God; (3) in a similar way, my powers of loving, too, will be focused for this amount of time solely upon God, and the response which I will be able to make is all the more intense and intimate because the demand for such a response is so single.   [20]

5. The makeup of the Exercises is rather simple. The basic division is into four parts, called "Weeks," although there are no fixed number of days within these respective "Weeks." The First Week is set in the context of God's love and its rejection by each of us through sin. The Second Week centers on the life of Jesus, from its beginnings through his public ministry. The Third Week fixes upon that very special time of Jesus' life—his passion and death. The Fourth Week looks upon the Risen Christ and the world which has been renewed in his victory.   [4]

We move from Week to Week according to the grace which God gives to us. Some persons come to an appreciation of a certain mystery of God's dealing with themselves more rapidly than others. For each person, it is the director who determines whether the time of the Week should be shortened or lengthened according to the movements of God's grace and each one's

Divine Majesty may make use of his person and of all he has according   to His most Holy Will.

[6]   **Sixth Annotation.** The sixth: When he who is giving the Exercises sees that no spiritual movements, such as consolations or desolations, come to the soul of him who is exercising himself, and that he is not moved by different spirits, he ought to inquire carefully of him about the Exercises, whether he does them at their appointed times, and how. So too of the Additions, whether he observes them with diligence. Let him ask in detail about each of these things.

Consolation and desolation are spoken of in [316, 317]; the Additions in [73-90].

[7]   **Seventh Annotation.** The seventh: If he who is giving the Exercises sees that he who is receiving them is in desolation and tempted, let him not be hard or dissatisfied with him, but gentle and indulgent, giving him courage and strength for the future, and laying bare to him the wiles of the enemy of human nature, and getting him to prepare and dispose himself for the consolation coming.

[8]   **Eighth Annotation.** The eighth: If he who is giving the Exercises sees that he who is receiving them is in need of instruction about the desolations and wiles of the enemy — and the same of consolations — he may explain to him, as far as he needs them, the Rules of the First and Second Weeks for recognising different spirits [316-324; 328-336].

[9]   **Ninth Annotation.** The ninth is to notice, when he who is exercising himself is in the Exercises of the First Week, if he is a person who has not been versed in spiritual things, and is tempted grossly and openly — having, for example, suggested to him obstacles to going on in the service of God our Lord, such as labors, shame and fear for the honor of the world — let him who is giving the Exercises not explain to him the Rules of the Second Week for the discernment of spirits. Because, as much as those of the First Week will be helpful, those of the Second will be harmful to him,

ability to respond. We note, however, that the full Exercises [11] should be completed in approximately thirty days.

6. When I as a retreatant am involved with the exercises of the First Week, I should not try to escape from total attention upon those considerations by looking to the areas of the later Weeks. At each stage of the retreat, I should work as if my whole response to God is found in the matter at hand.

7. In making the Exercises I should ordinarily spend one full [12] hour for each formal prayer period suggested by the director. When I feel tempted to cut short the hour, I should recognize the temptation for what it is—the first steps of taking back from God my total gift—and extend the time of prayer for a few minutes beyond the set time.

8. When I find prayer a joy, I may well be tempted so to pro- [13] long the period of prayer that soon I find myself responding to the consolations of God more than to God himself. At such times, the observance of the set hour is a safeguard against subtle self-seeking even in prayer. When I find prayer dry and even a burden, I must be sure to spend the full hour as part of my attempt to respond by waiting for the Lord.

9. If I feel a disorder in my attachment to a person, to a job [16] or position, to a certain dwelling place, a certain city, country, and so on, I should take it to the Lord and pray insistently to be given the grace to free myself from such disorder. What I want above all is the ability to respond freely to God, and all other loves for people, places, and things are held in proper perspective by the light and strength of God's grace.

10. I should be aware that the director, even if a priest, is not [17] necessarily my confessor. It is not essential for the director to know my past sins or even my present state of sin. At the same time, however, the attempt to speak out my temptations and fears, the consolations and lights given me by God, the various movements that happen within me, is the great advantage of a directed retreat, wherein the director can listen, sometimes enlighten, and adapt the progress of the retreat according to the way I am being led by God and responding to him. Without this openness between myself as a retreatant and the director, the retreat itself will not be able to be adapted and focused so as to lead to the growth which is possible for me.

as being matter too subtle and too high for him to understand.

[10] **Tenth Annotation.** The tenth: When he who is giving the Exercises perceives that he who is receiving them is assaulted and tempted under the appearance of good, then it is proper to instruct him about the Rules of the Second Week already mentioned. For, ordinarily, the enemy of human nature tempts under the appearance of good rather when the person is exercising himself in the Illuminative Life, which corresponds to the Exercises of the Second Week, and not so much in the Purgative Life, which corresponds to those of the First.

[11] **Eleventh Annotation.** The eleventh: It is helpful to him who is receiving the Exercises in the First Week, not to know anything of what he is to do in the Second, but so to labor in the First to attain the object he is seeking as if he did not hope to find in the Second any good.

[12] **Twelfth Annotation.** The twelfth: As he who is receiving the Exercises is to give an hour to each of the five Exercises or Contemplations which will be made every day, he who is giving the Exercises has to warn him carefully to always see that his soul remains content in the consciousness of having been a full hour in the Exercise, and rather more than less. For the enemy is not a little used to try and make one cut short the hour of such contemplation, meditation or prayer.

[13] **Thirteenth Annotation.** The thirteenth: It is likewise to be remarked that, as, in the time of consolation, it is easy and not irksome to be in contemplation the full hour, so it is very hard in the time of desolation to fill it out. For this reason, the person who is exercising himself, in order to act against the desolation and conquer the temptations, ought always to stay somewhat more than the full hour; so as to accustom himself not only to resist the adversary, but even to overthrow him.

[14] **Fourteenth Annotation.** The fourteenth: If he who is giving the Exercises sees that he who

B. *For the Director*

1. The director's role is that of helper. I help by explaining   [2]
the different ways of praying. I help by suggesting the matter
to be considered in prayer, and I do not hinder God's movements
in the retreatant by imposing my own interpretations of Scripture or of theology. The Exercises are, above all, a time for intimate contact between God and the retreatant, and the retreatant
will profit far more from the understanding and love aroused
by the grace of God than from the rhetoric or brilliance of me
as the retreat director.

2. I should expect that in the course of a Week the retreatant   [6]
will be moved in various ways. When the retreatant claims that
nothing is happening in prayer, I should ask how the retreatant
goes about his prayer, at what times he prays, where he prays,
and in general how he spends the day. Sometimes what appears
to be an action or event of small consequences can affect the
course of prayer for a whole day or a number of days. This again
is an area where I as a director can be a great help by the kind
of questioning which may uncover the cause that blocks the
openness to God's call.

3. When the retreatant is in a time of temptation or desola-   [7]
tion, I should be a kind listener and gentle support. To the best
of my ability, I should help to expose the ways in which the
powers of evil attempt to block the retreatant's ability to respond
to God. I should remind the retreatant that God continues to be
at hand even at such times with the necessary grace of strength
and light.

4. As the retreatant begins to be aware of the various move-   [8]
ments in himself, whether of consolation or desolation, I should
determine when it would be helpful to explain further the ways
for discerning the sources of such movement so ,that the retreatant is better able to understand how to respond to God.

5. Since there are different sets of instructions about the way   [9]
we are moved in the First Week in distinction to the Second
Week and thereafter, I should be careful to present and explain
only what is more immediately helpful to the retreatant for
where he is at present in his retreat. Otherwise, confusion can
result from the very explanations which were meant to be a
help.

is receiving them is going on in consolation and with much fervor, he ought to warn him not to make any inconsiderate and hasty promise or vow: and the more light of character he knows him to be, the more he ought to warn and admonish him. For, though one may justly influence another to embrace the religious life, in which he is understood to make vows of obedience, poverty and chastity, and, although a good work done under vow is more meritorious than one done without it, one should carefully consider the circumstances and personal qualities of the individual and how much help or hindrance he is likely to find in fulfilling the thing he would want to promise.

[15]   **Fifteenth Annotation.** The fifteenth: He who is giving the Exercises ought not to influence him who is receiving them more to poverty or to a promise, than to their opposites, nor more to one state or way of life than to another. For though, outside the Exercises, we can lawfully and with merit influence every one who is probably fit to choose continence, virginity, the religious life and all manner of evangelical perfection, still in the Spiritual Exercises, when seeking the Divine Will, it is more fitting and much better, that the Creator and Lord Himself should communicate Himself to His devout soul, inflaming it with His love and praise, and disposing it for the way in which it will be better able to serve Him in future. So, he who is giving the Exercises should not turn or incline to one side or the other, but standing in the centre like a balance, leave the Creator to act immediately with the creature, and the creature with its Creator and Lord.

[16]   **Sixteenth Annotation.** The sixteenth: For this — namely, that the Creator and Lord may work more surely in His creature — it is very expedient, if it happens that the soul is attached or inclined to a thing inordinately, that one should move himself, putting forth all his strength, to come to the contrary of what he is wrongly drawn to. Thus if he inclines to seeking and possessing an office or benefice,

6. In the First Week, it often happens that the retreatant will   [10]
be tempted to discouragement or rejection by thoughts about his
own unworthiness before God, the costs of such a loving response,
or fear for what others might think or say of him. I will find the
Guidelines for the Discernment of Spirits for the First Week, in
[314-327] below on pages 202-213, helpful to present at this time.
By contrast, in the Second Week, the temptation which the retreatant often faces comes more from the appeal and attraction
of some good, real or apparent. At this time, I will find the
Guidelines for the Discernment of Spirits for the Second Week,
in [328-336] below, more helpful.

7. I should be cautious when a retreatant is uplifted by con-   [14]
solation or fervor so that he desires to make great plans or to
pronounce some sort of vow. While I as the director should respect idealism, I must be able to weigh the gifts of God, along
with the natural endowments of personality, character, and intelligence, as I work with the retreatant.

8. I must always provide the balance for a retreatant, both in   [15]
times of exhilaration and in times of discouragement. I myself
am not the one who should urge a particular decision—for example, to enter religious life, to marry this or that person, or to
take a vow of poverty. My effort as director is always to facilitate
the movement of God's grace within the retreatant so that the
light and love of God inflame all possible decisions and resolutions about life situations. I should always remember that God
is not only Creator but truly *the* Director of this person's retreat;
I myself should never provide a hindrance to such an intimate
communication.

not for the honor and glory of God our Lord, nor for the spiritual well-being of souls, but for his own temporal advantage and interests, he ought to excite his feelings to the contrary, being instant in prayers and other spiritual exercises, and asking God our Lord for the contrary, namely, not to want such office or benefice, or any other thing, unless His Divine Majesty, putting his desires in order, change his first inclination for him, so that the motive for desiring or having one thing or another be only the service, honor, and glory of His Divine Majesty.

[17]   **Seventeenth Annotation.** The seventeenth: It is very helpful that he who is giving the Exercises, without wanting to ask or know from him who is receiving them his personal thoughts or sins, should be faithfully informed of the various movements and thoughts which the different spirits put in him. For, according as is more or less useful for him, he can give him some spiritual Exercises suited and adapted to the need of such a soul so acted upon.

[18]   **Eighteenth Annotation.** The eighteenth: The Spiritual Exercises have to be adapted to the dispositions of the persons who wish to receive them, that is, to their age, education or ability, in order not to give to one who is uneducated or of little intelligence things he cannot easily bear and profit by.

Again, that should be given to each one by which, according to his wish to dispose himself, he may be better able to help himself and to profit.

So, to him who wants help to be instructed and to come to a certain degree of contentment of soul, can be given the Particular Examen, [24], and then the General Examen, [32]; also, for a half hour in the morning, the Method of Prayer on the Commandments, the Deadly Sins, etc., [238]. Let him be recommended, also, to confess his sins every eight days, and, if he can, to receive the Blessed Sacrament every fifteen days, and better, if he be so moved, every eight. This way is more proper for illiterate or less educated persons. Let each of the Commandments be explained to them;

9. It is my role as a director to adapt the Spiritual Exercises to each retreatant, in view of his age and maturity, his education, and also his potential and his talents. I should decide what exercises would prove useless or even harmful to a retreatant because of a lack of physical strength or natural ability as well as what exercises would benefit and perhaps challenge a retreatant who is properly disposed and endowed. I may often discover that a retreatant at this particular time of life has neither the ability nor sometimes the desire to go beyond what is ordinarily described as the exercises of the First Week. So, too, I should make the judgment whether the full Exercises would be profitable to a particular retreatant at this time. Because the Exercises are a limited instrument through which God can work, I should be aware that many persons would not be able to enter well into the Exercises, perhaps because of a lack of natural talents, perhaps because of a certain kind of personality, or perhaps because God does not draw them to respond through the structured method of these Exercises.

[18]

and so of the Deadly Sins, Precepts of the Church, Five Senses, and Works of Mercy.

So, too, should he who is giving the Exercises observe that he who is receiving them has little ability or little natural capacity, from whom not much fruit is to be hoped, it is more expedient to give him some of these easy Exercises, until he confesses his sins. Then let him be given some Examens of Conscience and some method for going to Confession oftener than was his custom, in order to preserve what he has gained, but let him not go on into the matter of the Election, or into any other Exercises that are outside the First Week, expecially when more progress can be made in other persons and there is not time for every thing.

[19] **Nineteenth Annotation.** The nineteenth: A person of education or ability who is taken up with public affairs or suitable business, may take an hour and a half daily to exercise himself.

Let the end for which man is created be explained to him, and he can also be given for the space of a half-hour the Particular Examen and then the General and the way to confess and to receive the Blessed Sacrament. Let him, during three days every morning, for the space of an hour, make the meditation on the First, Second and Third Sins, [45-54]; then, three other days at the same hour, the meditation on the statement of Sins, [55]; then, for three other days at the same hour, on the punishments corresponding to Sins, [65]. Let him be given in all three meditations the ten Additions, [73-89].

For the mysteries of Christ our Lord, let the same course be kept, as is explained below and in full in the Exercises themselves.

[20] **Twentieth Annotation.** The twentieth: To him who is more disengaged, and who desires to get all the profit he can, let all the Spiritual Exercises be given in the order in which they follow.

In these he will, ordinarily, more benefit himself, the more he separates himself from all friends and acquaintances and from all earthly care, as by changing from the house where he

10. I may want to help a retreatant of talent and proper dis-   [19]
position through the full Exercises, but carried on in the face
of normal occupations and living conditions for the extent of the
whole retreat. As director I should determine, along with the retreatant, the amount of time possible each day for prayer and
divide up the matter accordingly. If an hour and a half can be
secured daily by the retreatant, the retreat could progress slowly,
with almost a single point providing enough material for such a
length of prayer. For example, in the First Exercise of the First
Week, each single example of sin might provide the matter to be
considered in prayer for that day. So, too, in the mysteries of
Our Lord's life, I may find it helpful to have the retreatant return
to the same mystery for three or four days in succession.

was dwelling, and taking another house or room to live in, in as much privacy as he can, so that it be in his power to go each day to Mass and to Vespers, without fear that his acquaintances will put obstacles in his way.

From this isolation three chief benefits, among many others, follow.

The first is that a man, by separating himself from many friends and acquaintances, and likewise from many not well-ordered affairs, to serve and praise God our Lord, merits no little in the sight of His Divine Majesty.

The second is, that being thus isolated, and not having his understanding divided on many things, but concentrating his care on one only, namely, on serving his Creator and benefiting his own soul, he uses with greater freedom his natural powers, in seeking with diligence what he so much desires.

The third: the more our soul finds itself alone and isolated, the more apt it makes itself to approach and to reach its Creator and Lord, and the more it so approaches Him, the more it disposes itself to receive graces and gifts from His Divine and Sovereign Goodness.

[21]

SPIRITUAL EXERCISES

TO CONQUER ONESELF AND REGULATE ONE'S
LIFE WITHOUT DETERMINING ONESELF
THROUGH [1] ANY TENDENCY THAT IS DIS–
ORDERED

[22]

PRESUPPOSITION

In order that both he who is giving the Spiritual Exercises, and he who is receiving them, may more help and benefit themselves, let it be presupposed that every good Christian is to be more ready to save his neighbor's proposition than to condemn it. If he cannot save it, let him inquire how he means it; and if he means it badly, let him correct him with charity. If that is not enough, let him seek all the suitable means to bring him to mean it well, and save himself.

[1] Without determining oneself through *is in the Saint's hand, the words being inserted between* life *and* tendency, *the word* without *being cancelled.*

SPIRITUAL EXERCISES [21]

The structure of these exercises has the purpose of leading a person to a true spiritual freedom. We attain this goal by gradually bringing an order of values into our lives so that we make no choice or decisions because we have been influenced by some disordered attachment or love.

PRESUPPOSITION [22]

For a good relationship to develop between the retreatant and the director and for the continual progress of the retreat, a mutual respect is very necessary. This may be especially true in areas of scriptural and theological presentation. A favorable interpretation by the director or by the retreatant should always be given to the other's statement. If misinterpretation seems possible, it should be cleared up with Christian understanding. So, too, if actual error seems to be held, the best possible interpretation should be presented so that a more correct understanding might develop.

[THE FIRST WEEK]

[23]   PRINCIPLE AND FOUNDATION

Man is created to praise, reverence, and serve God our Lord, and by this means to save his soul.

And the other things on the face of the earth are created for man and that they may help him in prosecuting the end for which he is created.

From this it follows that man is to use them as much as they help him on to his end, and ought to rid himself of them so far as they hinder him as to it.

For this it is necessary to make ourselves indifferent to all created things in all that is allowed to the choice of our free will and is not prohibited to it; so that, on our part, we want not health rather than sickness, riches rather than poverty, honor rather than dishonor, long rather than short life, and so in all the rest; desiring and choosing only what is most conducive for us to the end for which we are created.

[THE FIRST WEEK]

THE FOUNDATION: FACT AND PRACTICE [23]

God freely created us so that we might know, love, and serve him in this life and be happy with him forever. God's purpose in creating us is to draw forth from us a response of love and service here on earth, so that we may attain our goal of everlasting happiness with him in heaven.

All the things in this world are gifts of God, created for us, to be the means by which we can come to know him better, love him more surely, and serve him more faithfully.

As a result, we ought to appreciate and use these gifts of God insofar as they help us toward our goal of loving service and union with God. But insofar as any created things hinder our progress toward our goal, we ought to let them go.

In everyday life, then, we should keep ourselves indifferent or undecided in the face of all created gifts when we have an option and we do not have the clarity of what would be a better choice. We ought not to be led on by our natural likes and dislikes even in matters such as health or sickness, wealth or poverty, between living in the east or in the west, becoming an accountant or a lawyer.

Rather, our only desire and our one choice should be that option which better leads us to the goal for which God created us.

Note: This consideration is to be read over by the retreatant a few times each day during the first few days of the retreat. As is evident, these words express the basic Christian catechesis in the general terms of salvation. The prayer of the retreatant at this time may well be guided by scriptural texts which will enlighten and reinforce the notions contained in this foundation (see the suggested SCRIPTURE TEXTS, A, numbers 1-13, at [261], pages 154-155 below).

[24]

PARTICULAR AND DAILY EXAMEN

It contains in it three times, and two to examine oneself.

The first time is in the morning, immediately on rising, when one ought to propose to guard himself with diligence against that particular sin or defect which he wants to correct and amend.

[25]

The second time is after dinner, when one is to ask of God our Lord what one wants, namely, grace to remember how many times he has fallen into that particular sin or defect, and to amend himself in the future. Then let him make the first Examen, asking account of his soul of that particular thing proposed, which he wants to correct and amend. Let him go over hour by hour, or period by period, commencing at the hour he rose, and continuing up to the hour and instant of the present examen, and let him make in the first line of the G——— as many dots as were the times he has fallen into that particular sin or defect. Then let him resolve anew to amend himself up to the second Examen which he will make.

[26]

The third time: After supper, the second Examen will be made, in the same way, hour by hour, commencing at the first Examen and continuing up to the present (second) one, and let him make in the second line of the same G——— as many dots as were the times he has fallen into that particular sin or defect.

[27]

FOUR ADDITIONS

FOLLOW TO RID ONESELF SOONER OF THAT PARTICULAR SIN OR DEFECT

First Addition. The first Addition is that each time one falls into that particular sin or defect, let him put his hand on his breast, grieving for having fallen: which can be done even in the presence of many, without their perceiving what he is doing.

FOR A CONTEMPORARY READING

of these matters dealing with the Examen [24-43], see Aids for Prayer, F, The Examination of Conscience and Confession, at [24-26, 90], on pages 61-63 below.

———————

THE TEXT OF ST. IGNATIUS,
continued from page 24.

Second Addition. The second: As the first line of the G════ means the first Examen, and the second line the second Examen, let him look at night if there is amendment from the first line to the second, that is, from the first Examen to the second.

[28]

Third Addition. The third: To compare the second day with the first; that is, the two Examens of the present day with the other two Examens of the previous day, and see if he has amended himself from one day to the other.

[29]

Fourth Addition. The fourth Addition: To compare one week with another, and see if he has amended himself in the present week over the week past.

[30]

Note. It is to be noted that the first (large) G════ which follows means the Sunday: the second (smaller), the Monday: the third, the Tuesday, and so on.

[31]

G————————————————

G————————————————

G————————————————

G————————————————

G————————————————

G————————————————

G————————————————

[32]   GENERAL EXAMEN OF CONSCIENCE

TO PURIFY ONESELF AND TO MAKE ONE'S
CONFESSION BETTER

I presuppose that there are three kinds of thoughts in me: that is, one my own, which springs from my mere liberty and will; and two others, which come from without, one from the good spirit, and the other from the bad.

[33]   THOUGHT

There are two ways of meriting in the bad thought which comes from without, namely:

First Way. A thought of committing a mortal sin, which thought I resist immediately and it remains conquered.

[34] **Second Way.** The second way of meriting is: When that same bad thought comes to me and I resist it, and it returns to me again and again, and I always resist, until it is conquered.

This second way is more meritorious than the first.

[35] A venial sin is committed when the same thought comes of sinning mortally and one gives ear to it, making some little delay, or receiving some sensual pleasure, or when there is some negligence in rejecting such thought.

There are two ways of sinning mortally:

[36] **First Way.** The first is, when one gives consent to the bad thought, to act afterwards as he has consented, or to put it in act if he could.

[37] **Second Way.** The second way of sinning mortally is when that sin is put in act.

This is a greater sin for three reasons: first, because of the greater time; second, because of the greater intensity; third,

THE TEXT OF ST. IGNATIUS,
continued from page 26.

because of the greater harm to the two persons.

WORD   [38]

One must not swear, either by Creator or creature, if it be not with truth, necessity and reverence.

By necessity I mean, not when any truth whatever is affirmed with oath, but when it is of some importance for the good of the soul, or the body, or for temporal goods.

By reverence I mean when, in naming the Creator and Lord, one acts with consideration, so as to render Him the honor and reverence due.

It is to be noted that, though in an idle oath one sins more when he swears by the Creator than by the creature, it is more difficult to swear in the right way with truth, necessity and reverence by the creature than by the Creator, for the following reasons.

First Reason. The first: When we want to swear by some creature, wanting to name the creature does not make us so attentive or circumspect as to telling the truth, or as to affirming it with necessity, as would wanting to name the Lord and Creator of all things.

Second Reason. The second is that in swearing by the creature it is not so easy to show reverence and respect to the Creator, as in swearing and naming the same Creator and Lord, because wanting to name God our Lord brings with it more respect and reverence than

[39]

wanting to name the created thing. Therefore swearing by the creature is more allowable to the perfect than to the imperfect, because the perfect, through continued contemplation and enlightenment of intellect, consider, meditate and contemplate more that God our Lord is in every creature, according to His own essence, presence and power, and so in swearing by the creature they are more apt and prepared than the imperfect to show respect and reverence to their Creator and Lord.

Third Reason. The third is that in continually swearing by the creature, idolatry is to be more feared in the imperfect than in the perfect.

[40] One must not speak an idle word. By idle word I mean one which does not benefit either me or another, and is not directed to that intention. Hence words spoken for any useful purpose, or meant to profit one's own or another's soul, the body or temporal goods, are never idle, not even if one were to speak of something foreign to one's state of life, as, for instance, if a religious speaks of wars or articles of trade; but in all that is said there is merit in directing well, and sin in directing badly, or in speaking idly.

[41] Nothing must be said to injure another's character or to find fault, because if I reveal a mortal sin that is not public, I sin mortally; if a venial sin, venially; and if a defect, I show a defect of my own.

But if the intention is right, in two ways one can speak of the sin or fault of another:

First Way. The first: When the sin is public, as in the case of a public prostitute, and of a sentence given in judgment, or of a public error which is infecting the souls with whom one comes in contact.

Second Way. Second: When the hidden sin is revealed to some person that

THE TEXT OF ST. IGNATIUS,
continued from page 28.

he may help to raise him who is in sin — supposing, however, that he has some probable conjectures or grounds for thinking that he will be able to help him.

ACT [42]

Taking the Ten Commandments, the Precepts of the Church and the recommendations of Superiors, every act done against any of these three heads is, according to its greater or less nature, a greater or a lesser sin.

By recommendations of Superiors I mean such things as Bulls de Cruzadas and other Indulgences, as for instance for peace, granted under condition of going to Confession and receiving the Blessed Sacrament. For one commits no little sin in being the cause of others acting contrary to such pious exhortations and recommendations of our Superiors, or in doing so oneself.

METHOD FOR MAKING THE GENERAL EXAMEN [43]

It contains in it five Points.

First Point. The first Point is to give thanks to God our Lord for the benefits received.

Second Point. The second, to ask grace to know our sins and cast them out.

Third Point. The third, to ask account of our soul from the hour that we rose up to the present Examen, hour by hour, or period by period: and first as to thoughts, and then as to words, and then as to acts, in the same order as was mentioned in the Particular Examen.

Fourth Point. The fourth, to ask pardon of God our Lord for the faults.

Fifth Point. The fifth, to purpose amendment with His grace.

OUR FATHER.

[44]

GENERAL CONFESSION WITH COMMUNION

Whoever, of his own accord, wants to make a General Confession, will, among many other advantages, find three in making it here.

First. The first: Though whoever goes to Confession every year is not obliged to make a General Confession, by making it there is greater profit and merit, because of the greater actual sorrow for all the sins and wickedness of his whole life.

Second. The second: In the Spiritual Exercises, sins and their malice are understood more intimately, than in the time when one was not so giving himself to interior things. Gaining now more knowledge of and sorrow for them, he will have greater profit and merit than he had before.

Third. The third is: In consequence, having made a better Confession and being better disposed, one finds himself in condition and prepared to receive the Blessed Sacrament: the reception of which is an aid not only not to fall into sin, but also to preserve the increase of grace.

This General Confession will be best made immediately after the Exercises of the First Week.

FOR A CONTEMPORARY READING

of these matters dealing with General Confession [44], see Aids for Prayer, F, The Examination of Conscience and Confession, at [24-26, 90], on pages 61-63 below.

[45]   FIRST EXERCISE

IT IS A MEDITATION WITH THE THREE
POWERS ON THE FIRST, THE SECOND
AND THE THIRD SIN

It contains in it, after one Preparatory
Prayer and two Preludes, three chief
Points and one Colloquy.

[46]   **Prayer.** The Preparatory Prayer is to
ask grace of God our Lord that all my
intentions, actions and operations may be
directed purely to the service and praise
of His Divine Majesty.

[47]   **First Prelude.** The First Prelude is a
composition, seeing the place.

Here it is to be noted that, in a visible contemplation or meditation — as, for instance,
when one contemplates Christ our Lord, Who
is visible — the composition will be to see with
the sight of the imagination the corporeal place
where the thing is found which I want to contemplate. I say the corporeal place, as for
instance, a Temple or Mountain where Jesus
Christ or Our Lady is found, according to what
I want to contemplate. In an invisible contemplation or meditation — as here on the
Sins — the composition will be to see with the
sight of the imagination and consider that my
soul is imprisoned in this corruptible body,
and all the compound in this valley, as exiled
among brute beasts: I say all the compound
of soul and body.

[48]   **Second Prelude.** The second is to ask
God our Lord for what I want and desire.

The petition has to be according to the subject matter; that is, if the contemplation is
on the Resurrection, one is to ask for joy
with Christ in joy; if it is on the Passion, he
is to ask for pain, tears and torment with Christ
in torment.

Here it will be to ask shame and confusion at myself, seeing how many have

First Exercise [45]

PREPARATION: I always take a moment to call to mind the [46]
attitude of reverence with which I approach this privileged time
with God. I re-collect everything up to this moment of my day—
my thoughts and words, what I have done and what has happened to me—and ask that God direct it all to his praise and to
his service.

Note: This preparatory prayer, marking the beginning of each
formal prayer period, not only reinforces the continuing petition
for God's gift of reverence in me but also calls to mind how I
must continue to beg that my total day is by his grace more and
more integrated and centered in him alone.

GRACE: There is an importance in my speaking out the area [48]
of my need for God's grace according to the time, subject matter,
and my own dispositions during the retreat. Perhaps it may also
act as a preparation of my inner being for an openness to God's
entrance into a particular area of my life.

In this First Exercise, the grace I seek is the gift of feeling [47]
shame and confusion before God as I consider the effects of
even one sin as compared with my own sinful life. I may find it
helpful to imagine myself as bound, helpless, alienated as I
enter into these exercises dealing with sin.

been damned for only one mortal sin, and how many times I deserved to be condemned forever for my so many sins.

[49]   **Note.** Before all Contemplations or Meditations, there ought always to be made the Preparatory Prayer, which is not changed, and the two Preludes already mentioned, which are sometimes changed, according to the subject matter.

[50]   **First Point.** The first Point will be to bring the memory on the First Sin, which was that of the Angels, and then to bring the intellect on the same, discussing it; then the will, wanting to recall and understand all this in order to make me more ashamed and confound me more, bringing into comparison with the one sin of the Angels my so many sins, and reflecting, while they for one sin were cast into Hell, how often I have deserved it for so many.

I say to bring to memory the sin of the Angels, how they, being created in grace, not wanting to help themselves with their liberty to reverence and obey their Creator and Lord, coming to pride, were changed from grace to malice, and hurled from Heaven to Hell; and so then to discuss more in detail with the intellect: and then to move the feelings more with the will.

[51]   **Second Point.** The second is to do the same — that is, to bring the Three Powers — on the sin of Adam and Eve, bringing to memory how on account of that sin they did penance for so long a time, and how much corruption came on the human race, so many people going the way to Hell.

I say to bring to memory the Second Sin, that of our First Parents; how after Adam was created in the field of Damascus and placed in the Terrestrial Paradise, and Eve was created from his rib, being

THE SETTING: (1) the angels who rebelled against God.   [50]

It has been a deep part of our Christian heritage to understand that the first rejection of God's love in his creation is found among his special messengers, the angels. Theologically and spiritually, the sin of the angels exemplified the radical choice of self before God, which is the essence of sin, and the terrifying but necessary consequence of rejecting the very source of all our life and love. Pure spirits of decisive knowledge and totalizing love, the angels somehow were presented with the choice which God continues to give to each person he has lovingly made—whether we freely choose to respond to the life and love which he offers to us. Some angels chose to reject his free offer of love and life with him forever. Immediately by closing themselves off from God, they changed from a life of grace to a death-hatred of God and found themselves in their own choice of hell.

I mull over this sin in my mind, letting its decisiveness strike deep into my heart, and then I look to my many rejections of God's love.

THE SETTING: (2) the sin of Adam and Eve.   [51]

In the Biblical account of how sin entered into our world from the time of the first man, we once again get a picture of a very simple but direct rejection of God's love. Adam and Eve want to be as God is, and so they are described as eating the forbidden fruit of the tree of knowledge. Both try to escape the responsibility of the choice which each one has made by trying to shift the blame to someone or something else. The effect of this one sin is not only the loss of God's special sharing of his life in grace for all mankind, but also the continuing flow of evil perpetrated by men upon their fellowmen and their world.

I consider the effect of this first sin of man and woman for

forbidden to eat of the Tree of Knowledge, they ate and so sinned, and afterwards clothed in tunics of skins and cast from Paradise, they lived, all their life, without the original justice which they had lost, and in many labors and much penance. And then to discuss with the understanding more in detail; and to use the will as has been said.

[52] **Third Point.** The third is likewise to do the same on the Third particular Sin of any one who for one mortal sin is gone to Hell — and many others without number, for fewer sins than I have committed.

I say to do the same on the Third particular Sin, bringing to memory the gravity and malice of the sin against one's Creator and Lord; to discuss with the understanding how in sinning and acting against the Infinite Goodness, he has been justly condemned forever; and to finish with the will as has been said.

[53] **Colloquy.** Imagining Christ our Lord present and placed on the Cross, let me make a Colloquy, how from Creator He is come to making Himself man, and from life eternal is come to temporal death, and so to die for my sins.

Likewise, looking at myself, what I have done for Christ, what I am doing for Christ, what I ought to do for Christ.

And so, seeing Him such, and so nailed on the Cross, to go over that which will present itself.

[54] The Colloquy is made, properly speaking, as one friend speaks to another, or as a servant to his master; now asking some grace, now blaming oneself for some misdeed, now communicating one's affairs, and asking advice in them.

And let me say an OUR FATHER.

themselves and for all their posterity. I let the destructiveness of evil become fully present to my attention. If one sin can wreak such havoc, what about my own sinfulness?

THE SETTING: (3) the person who goes to hell.   [52]

There is the possibility of a person making a definitive "no" as a response to God's love and ratifying that "no" even in death. By the "no" one has given to God, one has chosen self and therefore all the opposite of the love and life forces which can have their source only in God. One has condemned oneself to the death of hell for all eternity.

How can I measure the number of "no's" which I have spoken to God up to this time? What can I say to God about myself?

COLLOQUY: I put myself before Jesus Christ our Lord, present   [53]
before me on the cross. I talk to him about how he creates because he loves and then he becomes man out of love, so emptying himself as to pass from eternal life to death here in time, even death on a cross, that by his obedience of love given to his Father he might die for my sins.

I look to myself and ask—just letting the question penetrate my being:

In the past, what response have I made to Christ?

How do I respond to Christ now?

What response should I make to Christ? As I look upon Jesus as he hangs upon the cross, I ponder whatever God may bring to my attention.

I close with an Our Father.

[55]

SECOND EXERCISE

IT IS A MEDITATION ON THE SINS AND CON-
TAINS IN IT AFTER THE PREPARATORY
PRAYER AND TWO PRELUDES, FIVE
POINTS AND ONE COLLOQUY

Prayer. Let the Preparatory Prayer be the same.

First Prelude. The First Prelude will be the same composition.

Second Prelude. The second is to ask for what I want. It will be here to beg a great and intense sorrow and tears for my sins.

[56]   **First Point.** The first Point is the statement of the sins; that is to say, to bring to memory all the sins of life, looking from year to year, or from period to period. For this three things are helpful: first, to look at the place and the house where I have lived; second, the relations I have had with others; third, the occupation in which I have lived.

[57]   **Second Point.** The second, to weigh the sins, looking at the foulness and the malice which any mortal sin committed has in it, even supposing it were not forbidden.

[58]   **Third Point.** The third, to look at who I am, lessening myself by examples:

First, how much I am in comparison to all men;

Second, what men are in comparison to all the Angels and Saints of Paradise;

Third, what all Creation is in comparison to God: (— Then I alone, what can I be?)

Fourth, to see all my bodily corruption and foulness;

Fifth, to look at myself as a sore and

Second Exercise [55]

PREPARATION: I always come to prayer, conscious of the reverence I owe to my God. I beg that everything of my day He may direct more and more to his praise and service.

GRACE: In this Second Exercise, I ask God for the gift of a growing and intense sorrow, even to the depth of tears if it be his grace, for all my sins.

THE SETTING: I see myself as a sinner—bound, helpless, alien-   [56]
ated—before a loving God and all his gifts of creation.

Without the detail of an examination of conscience, I let pass   [57]
before my mind all my sins and sinful tendencies that permeate my life from my youth up to the very present moment. I let the weight of such evil, all stemming from me, be felt throughout my whole being.

To gain even greater perspective on my sin, I reflect that out   [58]
of me—one human person among the millions of men who live— so much evil, hatred, and death can come forth. What can I compare myself to—a sewer polluting the waters of the river of life? a walking contagion of diseases who continues to walk throughout my world, affecting it and my fellowmen without warning?

I feel the weight and horror of so many effects of my sinful acts.

ulcer, from which have sprung so many sins and so many iniquities and so very vile poison.

[59]   **Fourth Point.** The fourth, to consider what God is, against Whom I have sinned, according to His attributes; comparing them with their contraries in me — His Wisdom with my ignorance; His Omnipotence with my weakness; His Justice with my iniquity; His Goodness with my malice.

[60]   **Fifth Point.** The fifth, an exclamation of wonder with deep feeling, going through all creatures, how they have left me in life and preserved me in it; the Angels, how, though they are the sword of the Divine Justice, they have endured me, and guarded me, and prayed for me; the Saints, how they have been engaged in interceding and praying for me; and the heavens, sun, moon, stars, and elements, fruits, birds, fishes and animals — and the earth, how it has not opened to swallow me up, creating new Hells for me to suffer in them forever!

[61]   **Colloquy.** Let me finish with a Colloquy of mercy, pondering and giving thanks to God our Lord that He has given me life up to now, proposing amendment, with His grace, for the future.

Our Father.

I put myself before God, and look at the contrast: God, the [59] source of life, and I, a cause of death; God, the source of love, and I, with all my petty jealousies and hatreds; God, from whom all good gifts come, and I, with my attempts to win favor, buy attention, be well thought of, and so on.

I look at my world. Everything cooperates to continue to give [60] me life and strength. I look at the whole support system of air, warmth, light and darkness, products of the earth, works of men's hands—everything contributes to my well-being.

I think of the people who have prayed for me and love me. The whole communion of saints has interest in my salvation and actively works to try to help me.

Everywhere I look, the more astonished I become, seeing so much good coming in on me, while I issue forth so many evils.

COLLOQUY: How can I respond to a God so good to me in [61] himself and surrounding me with the goodness of his holy ones and all the gifts of his creation? All I can do is give thanks, wondering at his forgiving love, which continues to give me life up to this very moment. By his grace, I want to amend.

I close with an Our Father.

[62]

THIRD EXERCISE

IT IS A REPETITION OF THE FIRST AND SECOND EXERCISE, MAKING THREE COLLOQUIES

After the Preparatory Prayer and two Preludes, it will be to repeat the First and Second Exercise, marking and dwelling on the Points in which I have felt greater consolation or desolation, or greater spiritual feeling.

After this I will make three Colloquies in the following manner:

[63]

First Colloquy. The first Colloquy to Our Lady, that she may get me grace from Her Son and Lord for three things: first, that I may feel an interior knowledge of my sins, and hatred of them; second, that I may feel the disorder of my actions, so that, hating them, I may correct myself and put myself in order; third, to ask knowledge of the world, in order that, hating it, I may put away from me worldly and vain things.

And with that a HAIL MARY.

Second Colloquy. The second: The same to the Son, begging Him to get it for me from the Father.

And with that the SOUL OF CHRIST.

Third Colloquy. The third: The same to the Father, that the Eternal Lord Himself may grant it to me.

And with that an OUR FATHER.

Third Exercise [62]

PREPARATION: There is the usual prayerful reverence and dedication of my day, consciously recalled as I enter into this formal prayer period.

GRACE: As in the Second Exercise, I continue to beg our Lord for the gift of a growing and intense sorrow, even to the depth of tears if it be his grace, for all my sins.

THE SETTING: Rather than take up new subject matter for consideration, I should return to those thoughts and feelings which struck me forcefully from the First and Second Exercises. I review those areas in which I felt greater consolation or desolation or, in general, greater spiritual appreciation. The idea of the repetition is to let sink further into my heart the movements of God through the means of subject matter already presented.

In the midst of these considerations, a threefold colloquy is suggested, to show the intensity of my desire for God's gift of sorrow.

COLLOQUY:

(a) First I go to Mary, our Mother, that she may ask, on my [63] behalf, grace for three favors from her Son and Lord:

1. A deep realization of what sin in my life is, and a feeling of abhorrence at my own sinful acts;
2. Some understanding of the disorder in my life due to sin and sinful tendencies, that I may begin to know how to amend my life and bring order into it;
3. An insight into the world that stands opposed to Christ, that I may put off from myself all that is worldly and vain.

Then I say a Hail Mary or a Memorare, or the like.

(b) Next in the company of Mary, I ask the same petitions of her Son, that Jesus may obtain these graces from the Father for me. Then I say the "Soul of Christ" or some such prayer to Jesus.

(c) Finally I approach the Father, having been presented by both Jesus and Mary. Again I make the same requests of the Father, that he, the giver of all good gifts, may grant them to me.

Then I close with an Our Father.

[64]
FOURTH EXERCISE

IT IS A SUMMARY OF THIS SAME THIRD

I said a summary, that the understanding, without wandering, may assiduously go through the memory of the things contemplated in the preceding Exercises.

I will make the same three Colloquies.

[65]
FIFTH EXERCISE

IT IS A MEDITATION ON HELL

It contains in it, after the Preparatory Prayer and two Preludes, five Points and one Colloquy:

Prayer. Let the Preparatory Prayer be the usual one.

First Prelude. The first Prelude is the composition, which is here to see with the sight of the imagination the length, breadth and depth of Hell.

Second Prelude. The second, to ask for what I want: it will be here to ask for interior sense of the pain which the damned suffer, in order that, if, through my faults, I should forget the love of the Eternal Lord, at least the fear of the pains may help me not to come into sin.

[66]
First Point. The first Point will be to see with the sight of the imagination the great fires, and the souls as in bodies of fire.

[67]
Second Point. The second, to hear with the ears wailings, howlings, cries,

Fourth Exercise [64]

This period of prayer is meant to be a repetition again—sometimes called a summary or a résumé. The hope is that the mind becomes less and less active with ideas since the subject matter does not change, and as a result the heart is more and more central to the way I find myself responding. The prayer period itself will probably be less active on one hand, and yet on the other by the grace of God it will grow in intensity. The intensity of the prayer is concretized by praying once again in the manner of the threefold colloquy.

Fifth Exercise [65]

PREPARATION: The usual prayerful reverence and dedication of my day is recalled.

GRACE: I beg for a deep sense of the pain of loss which envelops the damned, so that if I were ever to lose sight of the loving goodness of God, at least the fear of such a condemnation will keep me from falling into sin.

THE SETTING: an experience of hell. [66, 67, 68, 69, 70]

St. Paul speaks of our being able to grasp the breadth and length and height and depth of Christ's love and experiencing this love which surpasses all knowledge (Eph. 3:18-19). At its opposite pole, I try to experience the breadth and length and height and depth of hell—the despair of facing a cross with no one on it, the turning out upon a world which has no God, the total emptiness of living, an environment pervasive with hatred and self-seeking, a living death.

I bring the whole of my being into the vividness of this experience. I let all the horror of sin which has been the fruit of my previous prayer periods wash over me in an immersing flood. In many ways, this setting is the most passive of prayer experiences; it is not a matter of thinking new thoughts or even of looking for new images, but rather building on the

blasphemies against Christ our Lord and against all His Saints.

[68] **Third Point.** The third, to smell with the smell smoke, sulphur, dregs and putrid things.

[69] **Fourth Point.** The fourth, to taste with the taste bitter things, like tears, sadness and the worm of conscience.

[70] **Fifth Point.** The fifth, to touch with the touch; that is to say, how the fires touch and burn the souls.

[71] **Colloquy.** Making a Colloquy to Christ our Lord, I will bring to memory the souls that are in Hell, some because they did not believe the Coming, others because, believing, they did not act according to His Commandments; making three divisions:

First, Second, and Third Divisions. The first, before the Coming; the second, during His life; the third, after His life in this world; and with this I will give Him thanks that He has not let me fall into any of these divisions, ending my life.

Likewise, I will consider how up to now He has always had so great pity and mercy on me.

I will end with an OUR FATHER.

[72] **Note.** The first Exercise will be made at midnight; the second immediately on rising in the morning; the third, before or after Mass; in any case, before dinner; the fourth at the hour of Vespers; the fifth, an hour before supper.

This arrangement of hours, more or less, I always mean in all the four Weeks, according as his age, disposition and physical condition help the person who is exercising himself to make five Exercises or fewer.

whole experience of sin in which I have immersed myself in the past prayer periods. It is akin to the passive way my senses take in sights, smells, sounds, feelings, as an automatic datum for my attention. I know that the total felt-environment of sin, in whatever ways it can be most vividly mine, is the setting for this period of prayer.

COLLOQUY: Once I have let the awfulness of this experience   [71]
sink deep within me, I begin to talk to Christ our Lord about it. I talk to him about all the people who have lived—the many who lived before his coming and who deliberately closed in upon themselves and chose such a hell for all eternity, the many who walked with him in his own country and who rejected his call to love, the many who still keep rejecting the call to love and remain locked in their own chosen hell.

I give thanks to Jesus that he has not put an end to my life and allowed me to fall into any of these groups. All I can do is give thanks to him that up to this very moment he has shown himself so loving and merciful to me. Then I close with an Our Father.

HELPS TO PROCEEDING IN THE FIRST WEEK   [72]

The model of exercises presented here indicates the way of proceeding in the First Week. The usual prayer pattern consists of five formal prayer periods of one hour each. Two presentations of matter are given—in the First and Second Exercises. The remaining three periods of prayer are meant to be less demanding of thought, simpler and quieter, and a deepening of what has moved me. The last or fifth period of prayer (traditionally called an Application of Senses) is meant to be least cognitive; it is an attempt to let all that has been my experience in the previous prayer periods to pour over me once again in one summarizing and totalizing experience, out of which I can once again speak to my God.

A typical day of the First Week could use the Five Exercises just as they are. Each day of the Week could continue to be a repetition of these exact same exercises. There is also the possibility of using various scripture texts to let God's word enlighten the experience indicated in the exercises. In this way, scripture texts may so be chosen that the experience of

ADDITIONS

TO MAKE THE EXERCISES BETTER AND TO FIND BETTER WHAT ONE DESIRES

First Addition. The first Addition is, after going to bed, just when I want to go asleep, to think, for the space of a HAIL MARY, of the hour that I have to rise and for what, making a résumé of the Exercise which I have to make.

just the First or Second Exercise may permeate the entire day for two or three days apiece.

In any case, the pattern of the day as well as of the Week is meant to be clear. Each day should begin with no more than two presentations of scriptural matter, with the succeeding repetitions allowing the prayer to grow simpler, quieter, and more affective. So, too, the First Week is seen as a progression from days of more active thought and turmoil of feeling to its closing days of deep sorrow, acceptance, and thanks to God my Savior. The First Week suggests all that is integral to the basic Christian conversion experience: "Repent and believe the good news."

There is also the possibility of including other matters for consideration in this First Week when it is judged that it will be helpful for a particular retreatant. Matter on death itself or judgment might be presented in a manner similar to the exercises indicated in the First Week or else in a scriptural way. The only norm for the presentation of further ideas is the good progress of the retreatant.

Although five exercises are suggested for the duration of the First Week, age, condition of health, and the physical constitution of the exercitant may indicate that four exercises or less may be more profitable. When five exercises are used, the retreat day is ordinarily patterned to begin with the first period of prayer at midnight. "Midnight" does not describe actual time, but rather indicates that the prayer period should be set after an initial experience of deep sleep, which for many people comes within some two to three hours of sleeping time. It is at this time when both body and mind are relaxed and quiet that the prayer period can be very fruitful. The other four periods of prayer can easily be spaced throughout the day.

Aids for Prayer   [73-

The purpose of these directions is to help us to be better   90]
disposed as we move into the formal prayer periods and so
to be more open to the movements of God within us.

A. *Recollection*

My whole day should be consistent with my prayer. There   [73]

[74]

Second Addition. The second: When I wake up, not giving place to any other thought, to turn my attention immediately to what I am going to contemplate in the first Exercise, at midnight, bringing myself to confusion for my so many sins, setting examples, as, for instance, if a knight found himself before his king and all his court, ashamed and confused at having much offended him, from whom he had first received many gifts and many favors: in the same way, in the second Exercise, making myself a great sinner and in chains; that is to say going to appear bound as in chains before the Supreme Eternal Judge; taking for an example how prisoners in chains and already deserving death, appear before their temporal judge. And I will dress with these thoughts or with others, according to the subject matter.

[75]

Third Addition. The third: A step or two before the place where I have to contemplate or meditate, I will put myself standing for the space of an OUR FATHER, my intellect raised on high, considering how God our Lord is looking at me, etc.; and will make an act of reverence or humility.

[76]

Fourth Addition. The fourth: To enter on the contemplation now on my knees, now prostrate on the earth, now lying face upwards, now seated, now standing, always intent on seeking what I want.

We will attend to two things. The first is, that if I find what I want kneeling, I will not pass on; and if prostrate, likewise, etc. The second; in the Point in which I find what I want, there I will rest, without being anxious to pass on, until I content myself.

are particular moments within the day that can be capitalized on to help bring this about:

1. As I go to bed, I briefly recall the area about which my prayer will center on the following day. I ask God's blessings on my efforts this coming day.

2. When I wake up, I should not let my thoughts roam at random, but once again I recall the direction of this whole day's prayer and ask for God's continual help. Insofar as I am able, I will find it an aid to keep myself in this recollected mood all the while I dress. [74]

3. As it has been noted in the description of the First Exercise and thereafter, a conscious recall of what I am about and whose presence I am in is most helpful at the beginning of each formal prayer period. This should be done very briefly, just to establish the sense of reverence and dedication which should pervade my prayer time. [75]

4. In a similar way, every prayer period is centered in what has been called a colloquy. *Colloquy* is a term that describes the intimate conversation between the Father and me, Christ and me, Mary or one of the saints and me, and so on. This conversation happens on the occasion of my putting myself as totally as I can into the setting of the prayer; I will find that I speak or listen as God's Spirit moves me—sometimes as sinner, sometimes as child, at other times as lover or friend, and so on. A colloquy does not take place at any particular time within the period of prayer; it takes place as I respond within the setting of the exercise. It is true that I should mark the actual end of the hour of prayer with a definite closure— usually the Our Father or some such common prayer is a reverent way of signifying the end of this formal prayer period. [54]

B. *Position*

1. Formal prayer can be made in almost any bodily position. Certain positions are more helpful for some people than for others, just as certain positions are more helpful at one time in prayer than at another. The important aspect of position is found in the criteria whether I can be at ease and yet attentive, reverent yet relaxed. And so kneeling, sitting, standing, prostrate are all potential positions for prayer. Walking, [76]

[77]   **Fifth Addition.** The fifth: After finishing the Exercise, I will, during the space of a quarter of an hour, seated or walking leisurely, look how it went with me in the Contemplation or Meditation; and if badly, I will look for the cause from which it proceeds, and having so seen it, will be sorry, in order to correct myself in future; and if well, I will give thanks to God our Lord, and will do in like manner another time.

[78]   **Sixth Addition.** The sixth: Not to want to think on things of pleasure or joy, such as heavenly glory, the Resurrection, etc. Because whatever consideration of joy and gladness hinders our feeling pain and grief and shedding tears for our sins: but to keep before me that I want to grieve and feel pain, bringing to memory rather Death and Judgment.

[79]   **Seventh Addition.** The seventh: For the same end, to deprive myself of all light, closing the blinds and doors while I am in the room, if it be not to recite prayers, to read and eat.

too, may lend itself to praying well if it can image the relaxation and reflectivity of the exercise. But walking often can become a restless pacing back and forth which may have its effect upon the restlessness of the prayer of my inner being.

The only restriction upon positions in prayer arises from my awareness that a certain position may be a distraction for others, for example, to lie prostrate in a church or public chapel, where my position would call attention to myself and hence should not be used.

2. Once I have adopted a position in prayer and my prayer is going well, I should not readily change position because again the outward restlessness or shifting of position can jar the inner calm of prayer. Often a certain rhythm of kneeling and sitting, standing or walking, is helpful according to the moods of reflection and intense begging within the exercise.

C. *Review*

1. After a formal prayer period is finished, I should review [77]
what happened during the past hour—not so much what ideas did I have, but more the movements of consolation, desolation, fear, anxiety, boredom, and so on, and perhaps something about my distractions, especially if they were deep or disturbing. I thank God for his favors and ask pardon for my own negligences of the prayer time. Often it is good to signalize the difference of this review of prayer from the prayer period itself by some change of place or position.

2. I should spend about fifteen minutes in such a review. I may find it very helpful to jot down the various reflections that strike me so that I can more easily discuss with my director what has been my progress from prayer period to prayer period of this past day.

D. *Environment*

My whole surrounding, as well as my own deportment, can contribute to the prayerful atmosphere of the retreat or detract from it. Some areas which I could pay special attention to are:

1. During the exercises of the First Week, I may find it con- [79]
ducive to a deeper entrance into the mystery of sin and evil

[80]   **Eighth Addition.** The eighth: Not to laugh nor say a thing provocative of laughter.

[81]   **Ninth Addition.** The ninth: To restrain my sight, except in receiving or dismissing the person with whom I have spoken.

[82]   **Tenth Addition.** The tenth Addition is penance.

This is divided into interior and exterior. The interior is to grieve for one's sins, with a firm purpose of not committing them nor any others. The exterior, or fruit of the first, is chastisement for the sins committed, and is chiefly taken in three ways.

[83]   **First Way.** The first is as to eating. That is to say, when we leave off the superfluous, it is not penance, but temperance. It is penance when we leave off from the suitable; and the more and more, the greater and better — provided that the person does not injure himself, and that no notable illness follows.

[84]   **Second Way.** The second, as to the manner of sleeping. Here too it is not penance to leave off the superfluous of delicate or soft things,

by setting my prayer periods in places which are dark and deprived of light—keeping my own room dark, taking advantage of the dimness of a chapel or church, and so on. In general, I restrict my movements during this week, avoiding the pleasantness of sun and beauties of nature, the better to focus my attention on the darkness and loathsomeness of sin.

I continue to adapt such directions as these to fit the particular mood of the prayer of the Week in which I am currently involved.

2. In regard to myself during the First Week, it is important [78] that I keep my attention on the matter at hand, and do not subtly seek for ways to escape and relieve the awfulness of sin which may be building up within me. I do not dwell on things which would give me joy and pleasure—whether friends, occupations, music, food, or anything else. Rather I keep my thoughts more focused on the serious side of life.

For the same reason, I do not try to find occasions to laugh, [80] knowing how often laughter can be the attempt to escape the uneasiness of a situation. So, too, I must be more conscious of not trying to look around for distractions; it is helpful to keep a certain modesty of the eyes—always with the intention [81] of aiding the singleness of focus within my whole prayer environment.

E. *Penance*   [82]

1. General Description

Penance must always be seen in terms of my love response to God. Penance can be divided into two kinds: interior and exterior penance. The more important is interior penance; it is the grace which is sought throughout the First Week and can be described as a deep sorrow for one's sins and a firm purpose of amendment, especially in terms of an ever more full-hearted response of love in God's service. Confession received its formal name of the sacrament of penance (now called the sacrament of reconciliation) because of these interior sentiments of the sacramental encounter.

Exterior penance properly flows out of the grace of interior penance. It consists in taking on a certain self-inflicted punish-

but it is penance when one leaves off from the suitable in the manner: and the more and more, the better — provided that the person does not injure himself and no notable illness follows. Besides, let not anything of the suitable sleep be left off, unless in order to come to the mean, if one has a bad habit of sleeping too much.

[85] **Third Way.** The third, to chastise the flesh, that is, giving it sensible pain, which is given by wearing haircloth or cords or iron chains next to the flesh, by scourging or wounding oneself, and by other kinds of austerity.

[86] **Note.** What appears most suitable and most secure with regard to penance is that the pain should be sensible in the flesh and not enter within the bones, so that it give pain and not illness. For this it appears to be more suitable to scourge oneself with thin cords, which give pain exteriorly, rather than in another way which would cause notable illness within.

ment, either through denying ourselves something or through some positive action, to concretize our regret and resolution about our failings in our love response to God and neighbor. There are times, however, when exterior penance does not flow out of grace already received, but rather I take on this kind of penance to signalize further my effort and prayer in begging God for the gift of interior penance. In this latter case, I must be very diligent in following the advice of my director. The reason why advice is important is that more penance is better for some, and less for others. When I am seeking a particular grace and I seem not to find it, it may be the time for working out with the director some alternating periods of days in which I practice some penance and days in which I do not. The counsel of the director is very important at this time since I can easily be taken in by the subtle deception of thinking I can force God's hand by my penance or, more generally, that I am the one who can bring about such a gift because of my penance. Another reason that the director should always be kept informed lies in the area of my own self-deception: (a) either I am too ready to try to escape from any penance by using all kinds of subterfuges, such as "it is medieval," "I am not strong enough," "it's not for me," and so on; (b) or I am not properly ordered in my use of penance so that I attempt too much fasting, or too many vigils, or try to take on certain discomforts with the result that my prayer begins to suffer or I so weaken myself in this way very gradually that I am not able to sustain the retreat. Working with my director, I may be granted the grace by God our Lord, who knows our nature far better than we do, to understand what penance is suitable for me and when are the more suitable times for doing some penance.

Ordinarily, just as in the positions of prayer, I do not make a change in doing or not doing penance if God's grace continues to be operative in leading me ever deeper into the exercises of the retreat. So, too, at certain times during the retreat, penance seems to be called for whereas at other times penance would add a jarring note to my prayer. In every case, the counsel of the director is most important.

2. Purpose of Exterior Penance

Three principal purposes for performing some exterior penance at certain times are:

[87]   **First Note.** The first Note is that the exterior penances are done chiefly for three ends:

First, as satisfaction for the sins committed;

Second, to conquer oneself — that is, to make sensuality obey reason and all inferior parts be more subject to the superior;

Third, to seek and find some grace or gift which the person wants and desires; as, for instance, if he desires to have interior contrition for his sins, or to weep much over them, or over the pains and sufferings which Christ our Lord suffered in His Passion, or to settle some doubt in which the person finds himself.

[88]   **Second Note.** The second: It is to be noted that the first and second Addition have to be made for the Exercises of midnight and at daybreak, but not for those which will be made at other times; and the fourth Addition will never be made in church in the presence of others, but in private, as at home, etc.

[89]   **Third Note.** The third: When the person who is exercising himself does not yet find what he desires — as tears, consolations, etc., — it often helps for him to make a change in food, in sleep and in other ways of doing penance, so that he change himself, doing penance two or three days, and two or three others not. For it suits some to do more penance and others less, and we often omit doing penance from sensual love and from an erroneous judgment that the human system will not be able to bear it without notable illness; and sometimes, on the contrary, we do too much, thinking that the body can bear it; and as God our Lord knows our nature infinitely better, often in such changes He gives each one to perceive what is suitable for him.

(a) Traditionally described, penance makes satisfaction for past sins. Knowing that we truly are body-persons, we have the experience of "the spirit is willing, but the flesh is weak." This is oftentimes true because of the very areas of sinfulness in our past. The taking on of a bodily penance is an attempt to bring about that oneness of my inner and outer being to go specifically against the traces and scars which sin has left in me. [87]

(b) In a similar way, I take on exterior penance as a concrete reminder to myself that I do have to exercise a control, especially as I perform penances that touch those areas of my life where little or no control has been shown in the past. By the grace of God, this example of control through the exercise of penance shows forth the growth of my own human freedom. [88]

(c) More directly relevant to the retreat, perhaps, I perform some exterior penance because of some grace or gift I desire very earnestly, and I want to involve the wholeness of my being in this request before God. Often when such grace is granted, for example, the gift of deep sorrow for one's sins in the First Week or the gift of anguish with Christ in anguish in the Third Week, I may then feel moved to do some penance to enter more fully into the mysteries about which I am praying. [89]

3. Kinds of Exterior Penance

Three principal ways of performing some exterior penance are:

(a) Eating: If we do away with what is superfluous, it is not penance, but temperance. We do penance when we deny ourselves something of what is proper and good for us. We should never do away with what is necessary for us since then we would be destroying the very purpose of our taking on penance—that we might better respond to God in the prayer exercises of the retreat. If any physical harm or illness results from penance in this area, we should be aware that it is not suitable penance for us. [83]

(b) Sleep: If we do away with the superfluous in what is pampering and soft, it is not penance. We do penance when we take something away in our manner of sleeping that is proper and good for us. Once again if we find ourselves too sleepy [84]

[90]   **Fourth Note.**   The fourth: Let the Particular Examen be made to rid oneself of defects and negligences on the Exercises and Additions. And so in the SECOND, THIRD and FOURTH WEEKS.

to pray or eventual illness results, we know that we have over-stepped the bounds of suitable penance. People truly differ in their sleep needs, and we should always try to get enough that will enable us to work full-heartedly in God's service.

(c) Bodily penances: There has been a tradition among [85] many religious groups to have commonly recognized bodily penances, such as the wearing of a hairshirt, the taking of a discipline or whipping oneself with light cords, and the wearing of some kind of blunt-pointed chain around the waist or arm or leg. These kinds of penances coming down through our Christian tradition still may point the way to profitable forms of bodily penance today.

It should be obvious that bodily penances are not meant [86] to cause wounds, sickness, and so on, but rather they are aimed at willingly sought-out pain or discomfort because I am moti-vated by love. The possible areas of taking on discomfort or seeking out inconveniences for penance are very numerous, and those are chosen as most suitable and safe forms of penance which we find make us more aware of our attempts to express our love for God and for our fellowmen.

F. *The Examination of Conscience and Confession*   [24,

1. Although the retreat is already an inwardly reflective time,   25, it is often found helpful to set aside a brief time about mid-   26, way in the day and again at the end of the day before retiring   90] in a formal review of how I have spent the day. Within the retreat, this examination of conscience is not so much aimed at reviewing the areas of sinfulness, but rather at the fulfillment of all those aids of position, recollection, environment, and so on, which are meant to integrate my day, more wholly fixing it on God. Since the Weeks as well as individual days within the Week may make very different demands for such an integra-tion, I will find this style of particular examination especially helpful in maintaining the proper spirit.

2. Some retreatants find that it is very useful to keep some   [27, sort of record of this particular examination both to compare   28, the noon and evening periods as well as the progress from day   29, to day within the Week. Others may find a written record too   29, mechanical and do not profit from it. The better progress of   30, the retreat is always the norm for use or non-use of a partic-   31] ular method.

3. The format of the particular examination can be the same [32]
as that style of prayer used for making a general examination
of conscience, whether practiced daily or at the time of confession. There are five points in this method of approach: [43]

(a) giving thanks to God our Lord for all the favors he
has given;

(b) asking the help of the Spirit to enlighten me so that
I may see my sin as he sees it;

(c) going back over the events of the day or of the time
since my last confession to see the sinful acts, whether in
thoughts, words, or deeds, whether of omission or commission,
and the tendencies or roots of such sinful behavior;

(d) expressing my sorrow and asking God's forgiving love
to heal me;

(e) praying for the strength of God's grace to help me
amend my life.

4. There usually develops a desire for the sacrament of [44]
penance as we enter deeply into the exercises of the First Week.
Not only should confession be encouraged, but it is well to
consider the advantages of a general confession at this time:

(a) While there is no obligation to make a general confession, at a time when I have let the full burden of my sinfulness weigh me down, I come with even greater sorrow to present to the Lord all the sin and perversities which are so deeply
a part of my person.

(b) Through means of prayer, I arrive at a far deeper insight into my sins and their malice. Because the grace of the
retreat has led me to this deeper knowledge and sorrow, I
come with greater fervor and openness to the healing power
of Christ in the sacrament of penance.

(c) It is good to make such a confession, whether it be
a general confession or not, somewhere towards the end of the
First Week so that I approach the sacrament not in haste or
turmoil over the recognition of my sins, but rather in accepting
myself as sinner, as one always in need of radical healing, and
as one who acknowledges that God alone is my Savior.

SECOND WEEK

[91]

THE CALL OF THE TEMPORAL KING

IT HELPS TO CONTEMPLATE THE LIFE OF THE KING ETERNAL

Prayer. Let the Preparatory Prayer be the usual one.

First Prelude. The first Prelude is a composition, seeing the place: it will be here to see with the sight of the imagination, the synagogues, villages and towns through which Christ our Lord preached.

Second Prelude. The second, to ask for the grace which I want: it will be here to ask grace of our Lord that I may not be deaf to His call, but ready and diligent to fulfill His most Holy Will.

[92]

First Point. The first Point is, to put before me a human king chosen by God our Lord, whom all Christian princes and men reverence and obey.

[93]

Second Point. The second, to look how this king speaks to all his people, saying: "It is my Will to conquer all the land of unbelievers. Therefore, whoever would like to come with me is to be content to eat as I, and also to drink and dress, etc., as I: likewise he is to labor like me in the day and watch in the night, etc., that so afterwards he may have part with me in the victory, as he has had it in the labors."

[94]

Third Point. The third, to consider what the good subjects ought to answer to a King so liberal and so kind, and hence,

THE SECOND WEEK

CHRIST THE KING AND HIS CALL [91]

PREPARATION: I take the usual time to place myself before God in reverence and to beg him to direct everything in my day more and more to his service and praise.

GRACE: I ask of our Lord that I might be able to hear his call, and that I might be ready and willing to do what he wants.

THE SETTING: There are two unequal parts in this consideration, the first one naturally leading to the more important second part.

1. In the first part, let me put myself into a mythical situa- [92] tion—the kind of story-truth of which fairy tales are made. I imagine a human leader, selected and raised up by God our Lord himself; every man, woman, and child of good will is drawn to listen to such a leader and is inspired to follow his call.

His address to all men rings out in words like these: "I want [93] to overcome all diseases, all poverty, all ignorance, all oppression and slavery—in short, all the enemies of mankind. Whoever wishes to join me in this undertaking must be content with the same food, drink, clothing, and so on, as mine. So, too, he must work with me by day, and watch with me by night, that as he has had a share in the toil with me, afterwards he may share in the victory with me." If a leader so attractive and inspiring and so much a man of God makes such a call, what kind of a person could refuse such an invitation? How could anyone not want to be a part of so challenging and noble an adventure?

if any one did not accept the appeal of such a king, how deserving he would be of being censured by all the world, and held for a mean-spirited knight.

[95]

IN PART 2

The second part of this Exercise consists in applying the above parable of the temporal King to Christ our Lord, conformably to the three Points mentioned.

[96] **First Point.** And as to the first Point, if we consider such a call of the temporal King to his subjects, how much more worthy of consideration is it to see Christ our Lord, King eternal, and before Him all the entire world, which and each one in particular He calls, and says: "It is My will to conquer all the world and all enemies and so to enter into the glory of My Father; therefore, whoever would like to come with Me is to labor with Me, that following Me in the pain, he may also follow Me in the glory."

[97] **Second Point.** The second, to consider that all those who have judgment and reason will offer their entire selves to the labor.

[98] **Third Point.** The third, those who will want to be more devoted and signalise themselves in all service of their King Eternal and universal Lord, not only will offer their persons to the labor, but even, acting against their own sensuality and against their carnal and worldly love, will make offerings of greater value and greater importance, saying:

"Eternal Lord of all things, I make my oblation with Thy favor and help, in presence of Thy infinite Goodness and in presence of Thy glorious Mother and of all the Saints of the heavenly Court; that I want and desire, and it is my deliberate

2. In the second part, I consider Jesus Christ our Lord and [95] his call. If a human leader can have such an appeal to us, how much greater is the attraction of the God-Man, Jesus Christ, our Leader and King! His call goes out to the whole of mankind, yet he specially calls each person in a particular way. He makes the appeal: "It is my will to win over the whole world, to conquer sin, hatred, and death—all the enemies between mankind and God. Whoever wishes to join me in this mission must be willing to labor with me, so that by following me in suffering, he may follow me in glory."

With God inviting and with victory assured, how can any- [96] one of right mind not give himself over to Jesus and his work?

Persons who are of great heart and are set on fire with zeal [97] to follow Jesus Christ, eternal King and Lord of all, will not only offer themselves entirely for such a mission, but will act against anything that would make their response less total. They would want to express themselves in some such words as these:

"Eternal Lord and King of all creation, humbly I come be- [98] fore you. Knowing the support of Mary, your mother, and all your saints, I am moved by your grace to offer myself to you and to your work. I deeply desire to be with you in accepting all wrongs and all abuse and all poverty, both actual and spiritual —and I deliberately choose this, if it is for your greater service and praise. If you, my Lord and King, would so call and choose me, then take and receive me into such a way of life."

determination, if only it be Thy greater service and praise, to imitate Thee in bearing all injuries and all abuse and all poverty of spirit, and actual poverty, too, if Thy most Holy Majesty wants to choose and receive me to such life and state."

[99]   **First Note.** This Exercise will be made twice in the day; namely, in the morning on rising and an hour before dinner or before supper.

[100]   **Second Note.** For the Second Week and so on, it is very helpful to read at intervals in the books of the Imitation of Christ, or of the Gospels, and of lives of Saints.

SUGGESTED DIRECTIONS

1. The above exercise should be considered in formal prayer [99] twice during the day. The rest of the day is free of set prayer periods.

2. During the Second Week and thereafter, it can be profit- [100] able to read some classic spiritual works or some biographies of holy men and women. Scripture, too, can sometimes be used, although it is not wise to read the Gospels since certain mysteries of our Lord's life and ministry may call forth responses from me that are not consonant with where I am in my formal prayer periods of the retreat. The director and the retreatant should work out this area of reading together so that no influences contrary to the movement of the retreat are unwittingly intro- duced through the reading material.

[101] THE FIRST DAY AND FIRST CONTEMPLATION
IT IS ON

THE INCARNATION

AND CONTAINS THE PREPARATORY PRAYER,
THREE PRELUDES, THREE POINTS
AND ONE COLLOQUY

[102] **Prayer.** The usual Preparatory Prayer.

First Prelude. The first Prelude is to bring up the narrative of the thing which I have to contemplate.

Here, it is how the Three Divine Persons looked at all the plain or circuit of all the world, full of men, and how, seeing that all were going down to Hell, it is determined in Their Eternity, that the Second Person shall become man to save the human race, and so, the fullness of times being come, They sent the Angel St. Gabriel to Our Lady ([262]).

[103] **Second Prelude.** The second, a composition, seeing the place: here it will be to see the great capacity and circuit of the world, in which are so many and such different people: then likewise, in particular, the house and rooms of Our Lady in the city of Nazareth, in the Province of Galilee.

[104] **Third Prelude.** The third, to ask for what I want: it will be to ask for interior knowledge of the Lord, Who for me has become man, that I may more love and follow Him.

[105] **Note.** It is well to note here that this same Preparatory Prayer, without changing it, as was said in the beginning, and the same three Preludes, are to be made in this Week and in the others following, changing the form according to the subject matter.

[106] **First Point.** The first Point is, to see the various persons: and first those on

The First Day and First Contemplation   [101]

The Incarnation

PREPARATION: I take the usual time to place myself before God in reverence and beg that he direct everything in my day more and more to his praise and service.

GRACE: I ask for the grace to know Jesus intimately, to love   [104]
him more intensely, and so to follow him more closely.

Preliminary Note: The following description is an attempt to point out some of the ways of entering into the style of prayer called "contemplation." The description in words can make it sound very mechanical. To remember that the act of praying is our single focus will pour life-blood into the dead body of words.   [102,
103,

THE SETTING: I try to enter into the vision of God, in his triune life, looking upon our world: men and women aimless, despairing, hateful and killing, men and women sick and dying, the old and the young ,the rich and the poor, the happy and   108]

the surface of the earth, in such variety, in dress as in actions: some white and others black; some in peace and others in war; some weeping and others laughing; some well, others ill; some being born and others dying, etc.

2. To see and consider the Three Divine Persons, as on their royal throne or seat of Their Divine Majesty, how They look on all the surface and circuit of the earth, and all the people in such blindness, and how they are dying and going down to Hell.

3. To see Our Lady, and the Angel who is saluting her, and to reflect in order to get profit from such a sight.

[107]   **Second Point.** The second, to hear what the persons on the face of the earth are saying, that is, how they are talking with one another, how they swear and blaspheme, etc.; and likewise what the Divine Persons are saying, that is: "Let Us work the redemption of the Human race," etc.; and then what the Angel and Our Lady are saying; and to reflect then so as to draw profit from their words.

[108]   **Third Point.** The third, to look then at what the persons on the face of the earth are doing, as, for instance, killing, going to Hell, etc.; likewise what the Divine Persons are doing, namely, working out the most holy Incarnation, etc.; and likewise what the Angel and Our Lady are doing, namely, the Angel doing his duty as ambassador, and Our Lady humbling herself and giving thanks to the Divine Majesty; and then to reflect in order to draw some profit from each of these things.

[109]   **Colloquy.** At the end a Colloquy is to be made, thinking what I ought to say to the Three Divine Persons, or to the

the sad, some being born and some being laid to rest. The leap of divine joy: God knows that the time has come when the mystery of his salvific plan, hidden from the beginning of the world, will become manifest.

This is the context of the Annunciation scene, which we find in the text of Scripture (Luke 1:26-38). I try to stay with the eyes of God, and look upon the young girl Mary, as she is greeted by Gabriel.

I let myself be totally present to the scene, hearing the nuances of the questions, seeing the expression in the face and eyes, watching the gestures and movements which tell us so much about a person.

I notice how our triune God works—so simply and quietly. A world goes on, apparently oblivious of the total revolution which has begun. I look at Mary's complete way of responding to her Lord and God.

COLLOQUY: As I find myself immersed in the setting of this [109] mystery of the Incarnation, I may want just to stay with Mary or with our Lord, who has now become man for me. Sometimes I may want to speak out my joy, my thanks, my wonder, or my praise. According to the light I have received, I beg for the grace to know and to be able to draw close to Jesus, my Lord. I close the prayer period with an Our Father.

Eternal Word incarnate, or to our Mother and Lady, asking according to what I feel in me, in order more to follow and imitate Our Lord, so lately incarnate.

I will say an OUR FATHER.

[110]

THE SECOND CONTEMPLATION

IS ON

THE NATIVITY

Prayer. The usual Preparatory Prayer.

[111] **First Prelude.** The first Prelude is the narrative and it will be here how Our Lady went forth from Nazareth, about nine months with child, as can be piously meditated,[1] seated on an ass, and accompanied by Joseph and a maid, taking an ox, to go to Bethlehem to pay the tribute which Caesar imposed on all those lands.

[112] **Second Prelude.** The second, a composition, seeing the place. It will be here to see with the sight of the imagination the road from Nazareth to Bethlehem; considering the length and the breadth, and whether such road is level or through valleys or over hills; likewise looking at the place or cave of the Nativity,[1] how large, how small, how low, how high, and how it was prepared.

[113] **Third Prelude.** The third will be the same, and in the same form, as in the preceding Contemplation.

[114] **First Point.** The first Point is to see the persons; that is, to see Our Lady and Joseph and the maid, and, after His Birth, the Child Jesus, I making myself a poor creature and a wretch of an unworthy slave,

---

[1] As can be piously meditated *is in St. Ignatius' handwriting and is inserted before* seated.

The Second Contemplation [110]

The Nativity

PREPARATION: I take the usual time to place myself before God in reverence and beg that he direct everything in my day more and more to his praise and service.

GRACE: I continue to ask for the grace to know Jesus intimately, [113] to be able to love him more intensely, and so to follow him more closely.

THE SETTING: The familiar story of the Nativity should allow me the more easily to be present fully to the persons and places [111, of this mystery. Whatever methods help me enter into the whole 112, scene and to be with the persons involved I should embrace. 114,

To be able to enter into the deep-down stillness of this night, 115, to be able to see this very human baby with all the wonder 116]

looking at them and serving them in their needs, with all possible respect and reverence, as if I found myself present; and then to reflect on myself in order to draw some profit.

[115]   **Second Point.** The second, to look, mark and contemplate what they are saying, and, reflecting on myself, to draw some profit.

[116]   **Third Point.** The third, to look and consider what they are doing, as going a journey and laboring, that the Lord may be born in the greatest poverty; and as a termination of so many labors — of hunger, of thirst, of heat and of cold, of injuries and affronts — that He may die on the Cross; and all this for me: then reflecting, to draw some spiritual profit.

[117]   **Colloquy.** I will finish with a Colloquy as in the preceding Contemplation, and with an OUR FATHER.

[118]   THE THIRD CONTEMPLATION

              WILL BE A REPETITION OF THE FIRST AND
                     SECOND EXERCISE

After the Preparatory Prayer and the three Preludes, the repetition of the first and second Exercise will be made, noting always some more principal parts, where the person has felt some knowledge, consolation or desolation, making likewise one Colloquy at the end, and saying an OUR FATHER.

[119]   In this repetition, and in all the following, the same order of proceeding will be taken as was taken in the repetitions of the First Week, changing the matter and keeping the form.

which comes from eyes of faith, to watch how Mary and Joseph handle themselves, their own response to God at this time—these are various aspects or focuses of the mystery to which I may find myself drawn.

I should take note of the hardship which is already so much a part of Jesus' presence in our world. The labors of the journey to Bethlehem, the struggles of finding a shelter, the poverty, hunger, thirst, heat, and cold, the insults which meet the arrival of God-with-us—all this that he might die on the cross for me.

COLLOQUY: According to the different aspects which I may focus upon at any one time within the prayer period, I respond accordingly, for example, to Mary, Joseph, Jesus, the Father. Perhaps there is little to say because this style of contemplation is often more a "being with" experience than a word-response. [117]

I always bring the period of prayer to a close with an Our Father.

The Third Contemplation
A Repetition
[118]

This period is a repetition of the First and Second Exercises. After the preparatory reverence and dedication of my day, and the petition for grace, the matter from the First or Second Exercises, or from both together, is used. Quite often I find that I would like to return to a particular mystery in itself, such as the Incarnation; or I might find that in this Third Contemplation, the original first two settings flow one into the other. In making such a repetition, it is always important to return to those parts or points of focus where I have experienced understanding, consolation, or desolation.

Since the entrance into the setting of such a repetition is frequently very simple, the emphasis more and more is fixed on my personal response which is represented by the colloquy. I should always remember to close the prayer period with an Our Father.

In this repetition and in all those which follow, the usual manner of proceeding is observed as it was explained in the First Week. The subject matter is changed, but the same manner of repeating the exercise is continued. [119]

[120]

THE FOURTH CONTEMPLATION

WILL BE A REPETITION OF THE FIRST AND SECOND

In the same way as was done in the above-mentioned repetition.

[121]

THE FIFTH CONTEMPLATION

WILL BE TO BRING THE FIVE SENSES ON THE FIRST AND SECOND CONTEMPLATION

Prayer. After the Preparatory Prayer and the three Preludes, it is helpful to pass the five senses of the imagination through the first and second Contemplation, in the following way:

[122] **First Point.** The first Point is to see the persons with the sight of the imagination, meditating and contemplating in particular the details about them and drawing some profit from the sight.

[123] **Second Point.** The second, to hear with the hearing what they are, or might be, talking about and, reflecting on oneself, to draw some profit from it.

[124] **Third Point.** The third, to smell and to taste with the smell and the taste the infinite fragrance and sweetness of the Divinity, of the soul, and of its virtues, and of all, according to the person who is being contemplated; reflecting on oneself and drawing profit from it.

[125] **Fourth Point.** The fourth, to touch with the touch, as for instance, to embrace and kiss the places where such persons put their feet and sit, always seeing to my drawing profit from it.

[126] **Colloquy.** One has to finish with one Colloquy as in the first and second Contemplation, and with an OUR FATHER.

The Fourth Contemplation [120]

A Résumé

This period reinforces the notion of the repetition as outlined in the preceding paragraph. I might note how the prayer usually grows simpler in the matter considered, allowing always for a deeper and deeper personal response to the mysteries of Christ's life.

The Fifth Contemplation [121]

Application of Senses

Traditionally this prayer period has been described as an application of the five senses to the matter of the day.

After the preparatory prayer and the petition for the usual [122, grace, this last period of prayer within my day is meant to be 123, my own "letting go," a total immersion of myself into the mystery 124, of Christ's life this day. Just as when we tried to enter into the 125] experience of hell within the First Week, so here too, it is not a matter of thinking new thoughts or of trying new methods of getting into the mystery. Rather the notion is to build upon all the experiences which have been a part of my prayer day. Again it is akin to the passive way my senses take in sights, smells, sounds, feelings, as an automatic datum for my attention. The total felt-environment of the particular mystery of Christ's life, in whatever ways it can be most vividly mine, is the setting for this final period of prayer in each day.

COLLOQUY: I respond as I am so moved by God's grace. I [126] close with an Our Father.

[127]   **First Note.** The first note is to remark for all this and the other following Weeks, that I have only to read the Mystery of the Contemplation which I have immediately to make, so that at any time I read no Mystery which I have not to make that day or at that hour, in order that the consideration of one Mystery may not hinder the consideration of the other.

[128]   **Second Note.** The second: The first Exercise, on the Incarnation, will be made at midnight; the second at dawn; the third at the hour of Mass; the fourth at the hour of Vespers, and the fifth before the hour of supper, being for the space of one hour in each one of the five Exercises; and the same order will be taken in all the following.

[129]   **Third Note.** The third: It is to be remarked that if the person who is making the Exercises is old or weak, or, although strong, has become in some way less strong from the First Week, it is better for him in this Second Week, at least sometimes, not rising at midnight, to make one Contemplation in the morning, and another at the hour of Mass, and another before dinner, and one repetition on them at the hour of Vespers, and then the Application of the Senses before supper.

[130]   **Fourth Note.** The fourth: In this Second Week, out of all the ten Additions which were mentioned in the First Week, the second, the sixth, the seventh and in part the tenth have to be changed.

In the second it will be, immediately on waking up, to put before me the contemplation which I have to make, desiring to know more the Eternal Word incarnate, in order to serve and to follow Him more.

The sixth will be to bring frequently to memory the Life and Mysteries of Christ our Lord, from His Incarnation down to the place or Mystery which I am engaged in contemplating.

The seventh will be, that one should manage as to keeping darkness or light, making use of good weather or bad, according as he feels that it can profit and help him to find what the person desires who is exercising himself.

FURTHER DIRECTIONS

1. It is important to point out that throughout this Week and [127] the subsequent Weeks, I read only the mystery which is the subject matter of my contemplation. I do not read any mystery which is not to be used on that particular day or at that hour, so that the contemplation of one mystery does not interfere with another.

2. An ideal suggested order of the prayer day is: The First [128] Exercise on the Incarnation should take place at midnight (that is, after an initial period of sleep), the second in early morning, the third in later morning, the fourth in the afternoon, and the fifth in the evening.

The order of the prayer day has its importance in terms of the whole ordering process of one's life, which is the end of the Exercises.

3. The Second Week may well call for some adaptation in the [129] number of prayer periods. Whether the person is old or young, weak or strong, quite often the First Week has been a tiring experience. For that reason, it is often better not to use the midnight meditation time, with the possibility of either five or four periods of prayer spread out throughout the day.

4. It is probably obvious that some adaptation should be made [130] in terms of the aids for prayer.

Specifically, as soon as I awake, I recall the direction of this whole day's prayer, with the desire to grow in my intimate knowledge of Jesus Christ in order to love and serve him better.

Another help will be to recall at various times in the day the mysteries of the life of Christ our Lord from his Incarnation up to the mystery I am currently contemplating.

So, too, I as a retreatant use darkness and light, the chapel or the outdoors, insofar as I understand that it fits well with the mystery I am contemplating.

In regard to penance, again I conduct myself according to the mysteries under consideration. Some may call for penance, others will not.

And in the tenth Addition, he who is exercising himself ought to manage himself according to the Mysteries which he is contemplating; because some demand penance and others not.

All the ten Additions, then, are to be made with great care.

[131]   **Fifth Note.** The fifth note: In all the Exercises, except in that of midnight and in that of the morning, the equivalent of the second Addition will be taken in the following way: — Immediately on recollecting that it is the time of the Exercise which I have to make, before I go, putting before myself where I am going and before Whom, and summarizing a little the Exercise which I have to make, and then making the third Addition, I will enter into the Exercise.

[132]   THE SECOND DAY

Second Day. For first and second Contemplation to take the Presentation in the Temple ([268]) and the Flight to Egypt as into exile ([269]), and on these two Contemplations will be made two repetitions and the Application of the Five Senses to them, in the same way as was done the preceding day.

[133]   **Note.** Sometimes, although the one who is exercising himself is strong and disposed, it helps to make a change, from this second day up to the fourth inclusively, in order better to find what he desires, taking only one Contemplation at daybreak, and another at the hour of Mass, and to repeat on them at the hour of Vespers and apply the senses before supper.

[134]   THE THIRD DAY

Third Day. How the Child Jesus was obedient to His Parents at Nazareth ([271]), and how afterwards they found Him in the Temple [272], and so then to make the two repetitions and apply the five senses.

As a general reminder, I continue to observe very carefully all the aids for prayer which aim at the good progress of the retreat.

5. In a way of preparing myself similar to the preparation for the first prayer period of the day, I come to all periods of prayer in the following manner: as soon as I note that it is time for the next prayer period, even before moving on, I bring to mind where I am going, before whom I am to appear, and briefly recall the subject matter of the exercise. Then with a certain anticipation of God's gifts, I proceed to the usual preparatory reverence, as I enter into the very exercise itself.

[131]

The Second Day

[132]

On the second day, for the first and second contemplations, the Presentation in the Temple (see no. 35, at [268] below), and the Flight into Exile in Egypt (see no. 36, at [269] below), are used. Two repetitions, along with or including the Application of the Senses, are done as on the First Day.

Note: As was stated previously, sometimes it will be profitable, no matter how strong and well-disposed the retreatant, to make some changes in the first part of this Second Week, in order to attain better what is desired. So the first contemplation would be the one on rising in the morning. Then there would be one later in the morning, with another in the afternoon, and the final one in the evening.

[133]

The Third Day

[134]

On the third day, I use the contemplations on the Obedience of the Child Jesus to his parents (see no. 38, at [271] below), and the Finding of the Child Jesus in the Temple (see no. 39, at [272] below). As usual there follow the two repetitions, along with or including the Application of the Senses.

[135]   ## PREAMBLE TO CONSIDER STATES

First Preamble. The example which Christ our Lord, being under obedience to His parents, has given us for the first state, — which consists in the observance of the Commandments — having been now considered; and likewise for the second, — which is that of evangelical perfection, — when He remained in the Temple, leaving His adoptive father and His natural Mother, to attend to the pure service of His eternal Father; we will begin, at the same time contemplating His life, to investigate and to ask in what life or state His Divine Majesty wants to be served by us.

And so, for some introduction of it, we will, in the first Exercise following, see the intention of Christ our Lord, and, on the contrary, that of the enemy of human nature, and how we ought to dispose ourselves in order to come to perfection in whatever state of life God our Lord would give us to choose.

[136]   ### THE FOURTH DAY

MEDITATION ON

TWO STANDARDS

The one of Christ, our Commander-in-chief and Lord; the other of Lucifer, mortal enemy of our human nature.

Prayer. The usual Preparatory Prayer.

[137]   **First Prelude.** The First Prelude is the narrative. It will be here how Christ calls and wants all under His standard; and Lucifer, on the contrary, under his.

[138]   **Second Prelude.** The second, a composition, seeing the place. It will be here to see a great field of all that region of

INTRODUCTION TO THE CONSIDERATION [135]

OF

DIFFERENT STATES OF LIFE

One way of considering the mysteries of Jesus' early life is to see the interpretative direction in which they point. The ordinary life of the Christian is exemplified in Christ's obedience to his parents in the ordinary life of Nazareth. But the call to service in the Father's house is already manifested in the mystery of Jesus' remaining in the temple at the age of twelve to the consternation of his mother and father.

While I continue to contemplate his life, let me begin to examine myself and ask to what state of life or to what kind of life style is God in his loving providence leading me.

As a kind of introduction to this, in the next exercise, I consider the way Christ our Lord draws men and women, and on the other hand, the way the enemy of our human nature enslaves. At the same time I may also begin to see how I should prepare myself for a continued growth in whatever state or kind of life God our Lord may be moving me to choose.

The Fourth Day [136]

A Meditation on

TWO LEADERS, TWO STRATEGIES

We consider Christ, our Leader and Lord, our God and Brother, and we consider Satan, the personal enemy who sums up all the evils that beset mankind.

PREPARATION: I make the usual preparatory reverence and petition that God direct everything in my day more and more to his praise and service.

GRACE: I ask for the gift of being able to recognize the deceits [139] of Satan and for the help to guard myself against them; and also

Jerusalem, where the supreme Commander-in-chief of the good is Christ our Lord; another field in the region of Babylon, where the chief of the enemy is Lucifer.

[139]   **Third Prelude.** The third, to ask for what I want: and it will be here to ask for knowledge of the deceits of the bad chief and help to guard myself against them, and for knowledge of the true life which the supreme and true Captain shows and grace to imitate Him.

[140]   **First Point.** The first Point is to imagine as if the chief of all the enemy seated himself in that great field of Babylon, as in a great[1] chair of fire and smoke, in shape horrible and terrifying.

[141]   **Second Point.** The second, to consider how he issues a summons to innumerable demons and how he scatters them, some to one city and others to another, and so through all the world, not omitting any provinces, places, states, nor any persons in particular.

[142]   **Third Point.** The third, to consider the discourse which he makes them, and how he tells them to cast out nets and chains; that they have first to tempt with a longing for riches — as he is accustomed to do in most cases[2] — that men may more easily come to vain honor of the world, and then to vast pride. So that the first step shall be that of riches; the second, that of honor; the third, that of pride; and from these three steps he draws on to all the other vices.

[143]   So, on the contrary, one has to imagine as to the supreme and true Captain, Who is Christ our Lord.

---

[1] Great *is inserted, perhaps in the hand of St. Ignatius.*
[2] As he is accustomed to do in most cases *is inserted in the Saint's handwriting.*

I ask for a knowledge of the true life exemplified in Jesus Christ, my Lord and my God, and the grace to live my life in his way.

THE SETTING: There are two unequal parts in this consideration, the first one shedding light upon and giving direction to the more important second part.

1. To sum up all the forces of evil in the person of Satan makes me face the enormous power and oppression of evil itself. Keeping true to my own experience of the world, let me reflect how evil pummels the relations between nations and between peoples within a single country, so that no nation, no city, no state of life, no individual is left unscathed. I try to grasp the strategy of Satan as he attempts ever to enslave men and women and the world according to his design. People find themselves tempted to covet riches, and then because they possess some thing or things they find themselves seeking and accepting the honor and esteem of this world. From such honor arises the false sense of identity and value in which false pride has its roots. [137, 138, 140, 141, 142]

So the strategy is simple: riches (or "this is mine") to honor (or "look at me") to pride (or "I AM . . ."). By these three steps, the evil one leads us to all other vices.

2. Now let me look at Jesus Christ, who calls himself "the way, the truth, and the life." I notice how gently, but insistently, Jesus continues to call followers of all kinds and sends them forth to spread his good news to all people, no matter what their state or condition. Jesus adopts a strategy which is just the opposite of Satan: Try to help people, not enslave or oppress them. His method: Attract men and women to the highest spiri- [143, 144, 145, 146]

[144]   **First Point.** The first Point is to consider how Christ our Lord puts Himself in a great field of that region of Jerusalem, in lowly place, beautiful and attractive.

[145]   **Second Point.** The second, to consider how the Lord of all the world chooses so many persons — Apostles, Disciples, etc., — and sends them through all the world spreading His sacred doctrine through all states and conditions of persons.

[146]   **Third Point.** The third, to consider the discourse which Christ our Lord makes to all His servants and friends whom He sends on this expedition, recommending them to want to help all, by bringing them first to the highest **spiritual** poverty, and — if His Divine Majesty would be served and would want to choose them — no less to actual poverty; the second is to be of contumely and contempt; because from these two things humility follows. So that there are to be three steps; the first, poverty against riches; the second, contumely or contempt against worldly honor; the third, humility against pride. And from these three steps let them induce to all the other virtues.

[147]   **First Colloquy.** One Colloquy to Our Lady, that she may get me grace from Her Son and Lord that I may be received under His standard; and first in the highest spiritual poverty, and — if His Divine Majesty would be served and would want to choose and receive me — not less in actual poverty; second, in suffering contumely and injuries, to imitate Him more in them, if only I can suffer them without the sin of any person, or displeasure of His Divine Majesty; and with that a HAIL MARY.

Second Colloquy. I will ask the same of the Son, that He may get it for me of

tual poverty, and should it please God, and should he draw them to want to choose it, even to a life of actual poverty. Being poor, they will be led to accept and even to desire the insults and contempt of the world. The result will be a life of true humility.

Jesus' strategy is simple too: If I have been graced with the gift of poverty, then I am rich; if I have nothing, I have no power and I am despised and receive the contempt of the world; if I have nothing, my only possession is Christ and this is to be really true to myself—the humility of a person whose whole reality lies in being created and redeemed in Christ.

Through these three steps, Jesus and his apostles lead people to all other virtues.

COLLOQUY: Because of the importance of coming to some [147] understanding of the opposing forces of these two leaders and their strategies, I enter into the intensity of the prayer by addressing Mary, Christ, and the Father and begging favors from them.

(a) First I approach our Lady, asking her to obtain for me from her Son the grace-gift to be his apostle—following him in the highest spiritual poverty, and should God be pleased thereby and want to choose and accept me, even in actual poverty. Even greater is the gift I seek in being able to bear the insults and the contempt of my world, so imitating Christ my Lord ever more closely, provided only I can suffer these without sin on the part of another and without any offense to God. Then I say a Hail Mary or a Memorare.

(b) Next in the company of Mary, I ask the same petitions of her Son that Jesus may obtain these same favors or gifts from the Father. Then I say the "Soul of Christ" or some such prayer to Jesus.

(c) Finally I approach the Father, having been presented by both Jesus and Mary. Again, I make the same requests of the Father that he, the giver of all good gifts, may grant such favors to me. Then I close with an Our Father.

the Father; and with that say the SOUL OF CHRIST.

Third Colloquy. I will ask the same of the Father, that He may grant it to me; and say an OUR FATHER.

[148]

Note. This Exercise will be made at midnight and then a second time in the morning, and two repetitions of this same will be made at the hour of Mass and at the hour of Vespers, always finishing with the three Colloquies, to Our Lady, to the Son, and to the Father; and that on The Pairs which follows, at the hour before supper.

Note: This exercise is made three or four times within a single [148] day. The same three colloquies, with Our Lady, with her Son, and with the Father, close all the exercises as well as the one on the Three Types of Persons ([149-156] just below), which follows as the last (either fourth or fifth) prayer period of the day.

[149]

THE SAME FOURTH DAY LET MEDITATION BE
MADE ON

THREE PAIRS OF MEN

IN ORDER TO EMBRACE WHAT IS BEST

Prayer. The usual Preparatory Prayer.

[150]   **First Prelude.** The first Prelude is the narrative, which is of three pairs of men, and each one of them has acquired ten thousand ducats, not solely or as they ought [1] for God's love, and all want to save themselves and find in peace God our Lord, ridding themselves of the weight and hindrance to it which they have in the attachment for the thing acquired.

[151]   **Second Prelude.** The second, a composition, seeing the place. It will be here to see myself, how I stand before God our Lord and all His Saints, to desire and know what is more pleasing to His Divine Goodness.

[152]   **Third Prelude.** The third, to ask for what I want. Here it will be to ask grace to choose what is more to the glory of His Divine Majesty and the salvation of my soul.

[153]   **First Pair.** The first Pair would want to rid themselves of the attachment which they have to the thing acquired, in order to find in peace God our Lord, and be able to save themselves, and they do not place the means up to the hour of death.

[154]   **Second Pair.** The second want to rid themselves of the attachment, but want so to rid themselves of it as to remain with the thing acquired, so that God should come where they want, and they do not

---

[1] Not solely or as they ought *is a correction of* not only, *which is crossed out. The correction is perhaps in the handwriting of St. Ignatius.*

THREE TYPES OF PERSONS [149]

> This is a meditation for the same fourth day to
> aid me in my freedom of choice according to
> God's call to me.

PREPARATION: I take the time for the usual preparatory
reverence and dedication of my day.

GRACE: I ask that I may be free enough to choose whatever [152]
the lead of God's grace may indicate as his particular call to me.

THE SETTING: This prayer period is devoted to a consideration [150,
of three types of persons. Each one of them has taken in quite 151]
a few possessions—not always with the best of motives, and in
fact sometimes quite selfishly. In general, each one is a good
person, and he would like to serve God, even to the extent that
if these possessions were to come in the way of his salvation,
he would like to be free of them.

1. The First Type—"a lot of talk, but no action" [153]

This person keeps saying that he would like to stop being so
dependent on all the things which he possesses and which seem
to get in the way of his giving his life unreservedly to God. He
talks about the importance of saving his soul, but when death
comes, he is too busy about his possessions to have taken any
steps toward serving God.

2. The Second Type—"to do everything but the one thing [154]
necessary"

This person would like to be free of all attachments which
get in the way of his relationship with God. But he would rather
work harder or fast or pray more—really just do about anything
but face the problem which he feels holds him back in his relationship with God. He acts as if he is negotiating with God,
trying to buy God off. So though he may do many good things,
he keeps running from the better and more honest way to face
the issue.

decide to leave it in order to go to God, although it would be the best state for them

[155]   **Third Pair.**   The third want to rid themselves of the attachment, but want so to rid themselves of it that they have even no liking for it, to keep the thing acquired or not to keep it, but only want to want it or not want it according as God our Lord will put in their will and as will appear to them better for the service and praise of His Divine Majesty ; and meanwhile they want to reckon that they quit it all in attachment, forcing themselves not to want that or any other thing, unless only the service of God our Lord move them: so that the desire of being better able to serve God our Lord moves them to take the thing or leave it.

[156]   **Three Colloquies.**   I will make the same three Colloquies which were made in the Contemplation preceding, on the Two Standards.

[157]   **Note.**   It is to be noted that when we feel a tendency or repugnance against actual poverty, when we are not indifferent to poverty or riches, it is very helpful, in order to crush such disordered tendency, to ask in the Colloquies (although it be against the flesh) that the Lord should choose one to actual poverty, and that one wants, asks and begs it, if only it be the service and praise of His Divine Goodness.

[158]   THE FIFTH DAY

Fifth Day.   Contemplation on the Departure of Christ our Lord from Nazareth to the River Jordan, and how He was baptized ([273]).

[159]   **First Note.**   This Contemplation will be made once at midnight and a second time in the morning, and two repetitions on it at the hour of Mass and Vespers, and the five senses

3. The Third Type—"to do Your will is my desire" [155]

This person would like to be rid of any attachment which gets in the way of God's call to further life. His whole effort is to be in balance, ready to move in any direction that the call from God may take him. Whatever seems better for the service and praise of God our Lord is his whole desire and choice. Meanwhile, he strives to act in such a way that he seemingly is free of any attachments. He makes efforts neither to want to retain his possessions nor to want to give them away, unless the service and praise of God our Lord is the God-given motivation for his action. As a result, the graced desire to be better able to serve God our Lord is the cause of his accepting or letting go of anything.

COLLOQUY: I make use of the same three colloquies described in the preceding meditation on the Two Leaders, Two Strategies. [156]

Note: We may find it helpful at this time of the retreat when we might discover some attachment opposed to actual poverty or a repugnance to it, or when we are not indifferent to poverty and riches, to come to Jesus our Lord in prayer and beg him to choose us to serve him in actual poverty. We should beg with a certain insistence, and we should plead for it—but always wanting what God wants for us. [157]

The Fifth Day [158]

The contemplation on Our Lord's Baptism by John in the Jordan (see no. 40 at [273] below).

FURTHER DIRECTIONS

1. Beginning with the Fifth Day, it is suggested that only one Scripture passage be used to provide the prayer material for the entire day. Since the Exercises have as a primary aim the choice of a state or way of life, the purpose in limiting the amount of new material to be considered in prayer is to keep the head less occupied with many thoughts. Within the free time of these days, retreatants may likely be doing much weighing of alternatives, trying to understand the lead of God in their lives. As a result, the director is encouraged to keep the prayer material itself simple and less demanding of much reasoning. [159]

will be applied on it before supper; in each of these five Exercises, putting first the usual Preparatory Prayer and the three Preludes, as all this was explained in the Contemplation of the Incarnation and of the Nativity; and finishing with the three Colloquies of the three Pairs, or according to the note which follows after the Pairs.

[160]   **Second Note.** The Particular Examen, after dinner and after supper, will be made on the faults and negligences about the Exercises and Additions of this day; and so in the days that follow.

[161]   THE SIXTH DAY

Sixth Day. Contemplation how Christ our Lord went forth from the River Jordan to the Desert inclusive, taking the same form in everything as on the fifth.

THE SEVENTH DAY

Seventh Day. How St. Andrew and others followed Christ our Lord ([275]).

THE EIGHTH DAY

Eighth Day. On the Sermon on the Mount, which is on the Eight Beatitudes ([278]).

THE NINTH DAY

Ninth Day. How Christ our Lord appeared to His disciples on the waves of the sea ([280]).

THE TENTH DAY

Tenth Day. How the Lord preached in the[1] Temple ([288]).

THE ELEVENTH DAY

Eleventh Day. On the raising of Lazarus ([285]).

---

[1] In the *is in the Saint's hand, over a word erased.*

Yet it should be pointed out that the number of prayer periods is maintained, with the usual repetitions leading to the more simple gaze of the Application of the Senses for the same mystery of Christ's life.

It might also be good to recall that even though we speak of a simplifying of the prayer at this time of the retreat, we are still most careful to observe the preparatory reverence and dedication of everything in our day to God, the petition for a specified grace, and the intimate conversation of the colloquy. Because of the intensity of the search for God's will and our response at this period of the retreat, the triple colloquy addressed to Mary, Christ, and the Father might well remain an ordinary part of these prayer periods.

2. The Particular Examen of Conscience usually made at midday and before retiring should continue its focus on the faults and negligences with regard to the exercises of the day, especially in view of the helps or aids to prayers which have been suggested. [160]

The Sixth Day [161]

The contemplation on Christ our Lord's being led into the desert to be tempted (see no. 41 at [274] below).

The Seventh Day

The contemplation on Jesus' calls to the apostles (see no. 42 at [275] below).

The Eighth Day

The contemplation on the Eight Beatitudes (see no. 45 at [272] below).

The Ninth Day

The contemplation on Christ's walking on the water (see no. 47 at [280] below).

THE TWELFTH DAY

Twelfth Day. On Palm Sunday ([287]).

[162]   **First Note.** The first note is that in the Contemplations of this Second Week, according to the time each one wants to spend, or according as he gets profit, he can lengthen or shorten: if he lengthens, taking the Mysteries of the Visitation of Our Lady to St. Elizabeth, the Shepherds, the Circumcision of the Child Jesus, and the Three Kings, and so of others; and if he shortens, he can even omit some of those which are set down. Because this is to give an introduction and way to contemplate better and more completely afterwards.

[163]   **Second Note.** The second: The matter of the Elections will be begun from the Contemplation on Nazareth to the Jordan, taken inclusively, which is the fifth day, as is explained in the following.

[164]   **Third Note.** The third: Before entering on the Elections, that a man may get attachment to the true doctrine of Christ our Lord, it is very helpful to consider and mark the following three Manners of Humility, reflecting on them occasionally through all the day, and also making the Colloquies, as will be said later.

The Tenth Day

The contemplation on Jesus preaching in the temple (see no. 55 at [288] below).

The Eleventh Day

The contemplation on Jesus' raising of Lazarus (see no. 52 at [285] below).

The Twelfth Day

The contemplation on the triumphal entry into Jerusalem (see no. 54 at [287] below).

FURTHER DIRECTIONS

1. The Second Week, similar to the First, has no set number [162] of days. According to the progress of the retreatant, especially in view of a choice which one is trying to clarify, the director may want to lengthen or shorten the Week.

In lengthening the Week, the director might suggest other mysteries from the infancy narratives in the Gospels, such as the Visitation of Mary to Elizabeth, the Shepherds at Bethlehem, the Circumcision of the Child Jesus, and the Three Wise Men's Journey and Adoration. By contrast, if the director thinks it well that the Week should be shortened, he may omit some of the mysteries that have been proposed. However many mysteries are taken up in the Second Week, they only serve to introduce the retreatant into a way of prayer which will continue to draw a person more deeply into the life of Christ our Lord.

2. If a retreatant is trying to clarify a choice of a state or [163] way of life, the time for this consideration begins with the Fifth Day, where the contemplation of Our Lord's own setting forth to the Jordan determines the vocation of his own public life.

3. Before I as a retreatant enter into my considerations about [164] the choice of a state or way of life, it is very useful to spend some time mulling over the following description of Three Kinds of Humility. These are thought over from time to time outside of the formal prayer periods from the Fifth Day onward. Perhaps after a day or two of consideration, I may find that I want

[165] **First Humility.** The first manner of Humility is necessary for eternal salvation; namely, that I so lower and so humble myself, as much as is possible to me, that in everything I obey the law of God, so that, even if they made me lord of all the created things in this world, nor for my own temporal life, I would not be in deliberation about breaking a Commandment, whether Divine or human, which binds me under mortal sin.

[166] **Second Humility.** The second is more perfect Humility than the first; namely, if I find myself at such a stage that I do not want, and feel no inclination to have, riches rather than poverty, to want honor rather than dishonor, to desire a long rather than a short life — the service of God our Lord and the salvation of my soul being equal; and so not for all creation, nor because they would take away my life, would I be in deliberation about committing a venial sin.

[167] **Third Humility.** The third is most perfect Humility; namely, when — including the first and second, and the praise and glory of the Divine Majesty being equal — in order to imitate and be more actually like Christ our Lord, I want and choose poverty with Christ poor rather than riches, opprobrium with Christ replete with it rather than honors; and to desire to be rated as worthless and a fool for Christ, Who first was held as such, rather than wise or prudent in this world.

to be gifted in the way most expressive of my love and dedication to Jesus Christ, my Lord and God. Then I should make use of the threefold colloquy to manifest the intensity of my desire for this grace.

THREE KINDS OF HUMILITY

Humility lies in the acceptance of Jesus Christ as the fullness of what it means to be human. To be humble is to live as close to the truth as possible: that I am created to the likeness of Christ, that I am meant to live according to the pattern of his paschal mystery, and that my whole fulfillment is found in being as near to Christ as he draws me to himself. The following descriptions try to sum up three different general areas on the spectrum of humility as it is actually lived by men and women.

1. The First Kind of Humility. This is living out the truth which is necessary for salvation, and so it describes one extreme of the spectrum. I would want to do nothing that would cut me off from God—not even were I made head of all creation or even just to save my own life here on earth. I know that grave sin in this sense is to miss the whole meaning of being a person— one who is created and redeemed and is destined to live forever in love with God my Creator and Lord. [165]

2. The Second Kind of Humility. This kind is more perfect than the first, and so we find ourselves somewhere along the middle of the spectrum. My life is firmly grounded in the fact that the reality of being a person is seen fully in Jesus Christ. Just as "I have come to do your will, O God" is the motivating force of his life, so the only real principle of choice in my life is to seek out and do the will of my Father. With this habitual attitude, I find that I can maintain a certain balance in my inclinations to have riches rather than poverty, honor rather than dishonor, or to desire a long life rather than a short life. I would not want to turn away from God even in small ways, because my whole desire is to respond ever more faithfully to his call. [166]

3. The Third Kind of Humility. This is close to the other end of the spectrum, since it demands the understanding and action of a greater grace-gift. It consists in this. I so much want the truth of Christ's life to be fully the truth of my own that I find myself, moved by grace, with a love and a desire for poverty in order to be with the poor Christ; a love and a desire for insults [167]

[168]   **Note.** So, it is very helpful for whoever desires to get this third Humility, to make the three already mentioned Colloquies of THE PAIRS, asking that Our Lord would be pleased to choose him·to this third greater and better Humility, in order more to imitate and serve Him, if it be equal or greater service and praise to His Divine Majesty.

[169]   ## PRELUDE FOR MAKING ELECTION

First Point. In every good election, as far as depends on us, the eye of our intention ought to be simple, only looking at what we are created for, namely, the praise of God our Lord and the salvation of our soul. And so I ought to choose whatever I do, that it may help me for the end for which I am created, not ordering or bringing the end to the means, but the means to the end: as it happens that many choose first to marry — which is a means — and secondarily to serve God our Lord in the married life — which service of God is the end. So, too, there are others who first want to have benefices, and then to serve God in them. So that those do not go straight to God, but want God to come straight to their disordered tendencies, and consequently they make a means of the end, and an end of the means. So that what they had to take first, they take last; because first we have to set as our aim the wanting to serve God, — which is the end, —and secondarily, to take a benefice, or to marry, if it is more suitable to us, — which is the means for the end. So, nothing ought to move me to take such means or to deprive myself of them, except only the service and praise of God our Lord and the eternal salvation of my soul.

in order to be closer to Christ in his own rejection by people; a love and a desire to be considered worthless and a fool for Christ, rather than to be esteemed as wise and prudent according to the standards of the world. By grace, I find myself so moved to follow Jesus Christ in the most intimate union possible, that his experiences are reflected in my own. In that, I find my delight.

Note: If after some time for consideration I as a retreatant [168] want to move more in the direction of this third kind of humility, it will help much to make use of the threefold colloquy, as it has been explained above. I should beg our Lord to choose me for the gift of this third kind of humility in order that I may find my own life more patterned according to Jesus, my God and Lord—always, of course, if this is to be for the greater praise and service of God.

INTRODUCTION TO MAKING A CHOICE [169]

OF A STATE OR WAY OF LIFE

In making a choice or in coming to a decision, only one thing is really important—to seek and to find what God calls me to at this time of my life. I know that his call remains faithful; he has created me for himself and my salvation is found in that love. All my choices, then, must be consistent with this given direction of my life.

It becomes obvious how easy it is for me to forget such a simple truth as the end and goal of my whole existence when I consider the manner in which choices are often made. Many people, for example, choose marriage, which is a means, and only secondarily consider the service of God our Lord in marriage, though to do the will of God is each person's end and goal. Many people first choose to make a lot of money or to be successful, and only afterwards to be able to serve God by it. And so too in their striving for power, popularity, and so on. All of these people exhibit an attitude of putting God into second place, and they want God to come into their lives only after their own disordered attachment. In other words, they mix up the order of an end and a means to that end. What they ought to seek first and above all else, they often put last.

It is good, then, for me to recall that my whole aim in life should be to seek to serve God in whatever way his call may

[170] TO GET KNOWLEDGE AS TO WHAT MATTERS
AN ELECTION OUGHT TO BE MADE
ABOUT, AND IT CONTAINS FOUR POINTS
AND ONE NOTE

First Point. The first Point: It is
necessary that everything about which we
want to make an election should be indifferent, or good, in itself, and should be
allowed within our Holy Mother the hierarchical Church, and not bad nor opposed
to her.

[171] **Second Point.** Second: There are some
things which fall under unchangeable
election, such as are the priesthood, marriage, etc. There are others which fall
under an election that can be changed, such
as are to take benefices or leave them,
to take temporal goods or rid oneself of
them.

[172] **Third Point.** Third: In the unchangeable Election which has already been once
made — such as marriage, the priesthood,
etc.— there is nothing more to choose,
because one cannot release himself; only
it is to be seen to that if one have not made
his election duly and ordinately and without disordered tendencies, repenting let
him see to living a good life in his election.
It does not appear that this election is a
Divine vocation,[1] as being an election out
of order and awry. Many err in this,
setting up a perverse or bad election as a
Divine[2] vocation; for every Divine vocation is always pure and clear, without
mixture of flesh, or of any other inordinate
tendency.

---

[1] It does *not* appear that *this election* is a Divine vocation *is in the Saint's hand, correcting* we can *not* say that *this
election* is His vocation.

[2] Divine *is added in St. Ignatius' hand.*

come to me. Keeping clearly before me my desire to serve God our Lord, I can begin to search out the means of marrying or not marrying, a life of business involvement or a life of simple frugality, and the like, for these are all means to accomplishing the end. I will choose to use or not use such means only through the inspiration and movement of God's grace leading me on in his service and to my own salvation.

MATTERS ABOUT WHICH A CHOICE [170]

SHOULD BE MADE

The purpose of these observations is to provide a certain basic information on the matters about which decisions are very important. It contains four points and a note.

1. When we are making a decision or choice, we are not deliberating about choices which involve sin, but rather we are considering alternatives which are lawful and good within our Catholic Church and not bad or opposed to her.

2. There are choices which represent permanent commitment [171] such as marriage, priesthood, and religious life. There are other choices which can be changed, such as a seeking after a successful career in business or medicine, or a decision to live according to a certain life style.

3. With regard to a permanent commitment already made, [172] our basic attitude should be that the only choice still called for is the full-hearted gift of self to this state of life. Only this is to be noted. If it becomes apparent that the choice or decision has not been made as it should have been and if there has been a certain disordered attachment involved, our first response is one of sorrow and an attempt to amend by putting our efforts into righting the situation. Professional help or the help of friends who can be objective, along with legitimate authority itself, must oftentimes play an important role at this time of reevaluation.

There is no sense trying to say God's call is directly involved in a choice which we have made because of a disordered attachment. For the call from God is not at the whim of faulty information, sensual emotion, or disordered love.

[173]   **Fourth Point.** Fourth: If some one has duly and ordinately made election of things which are under election that can be changed, and has not yielded to flesh or world, there is no reason for his making election anew, but let him perfect himself as much as he can in that already chosen.

[174]   **Note.** It is to be remarked that if such election that can be changed was not made sincerely and well in order, then it helps to make the election duly, if one has a desire that fruits notable and very pleasing to God our Lord should come from him.

[175]
THREE TIMES
FOR MAKING, IN ANY ONE OF THEM, A SOUND
AND GOOD ELECTION

First Time. The first time is, when God our Lord so moves and attracts the will, that without doubting, or being able to doubt, such devout soul follows what is shown it, as St. Paul and St. Matthew did in following Christ our Lord.

[176]   **Second Time.** The second, when enough light and knowledge is received by experience of consolations and desolations, and by the experience of the discernment of various spirits.

[177]   **Third Time.** The third time is quiet, when one considers, first, for what man is born — namely, to praise God our Lord and save his soul — and desiring this chooses as means a life or state within the limits of the Church, in order that he may be helped in the service of his Lord and the salvation of his soul.

I said time of quiet, when the soul is not acted on by various spirits, and uses its natural powers freely and tranquilly.

4. When we are dealing with matters which can be changed, [173] there is no reason to feel anxiety or to move to an unhealthy introspection if we seem to have come to the decision properly and in good order when we first made it. Our one desire should be to find our continued growth in the way of life we have chosen.

Note: If we have poorly come to a decision in matters that [174] are changeable, we should try to make a choice in the proper way whether it would be maintaining the same pattern of life or it would demand a change. For our desire is to praise and serve God in all our choices so that he can continue to work through us for the good of our fellowmen and our world.

THREE TIMES WHEN A CORRECT AND GOOD CHOICE [175]

OF A STATE OR WAY OF LIFE

MAY BE MADE

1. First Time. There is a time of clarity which comes with undeviating persistence. We think of the dramatic change in St. Paul on the road to Damascus, for once he began to respond to the Jesus whom he had been persecuting he never hesitated. From the brief description of Matthew's call in the Gospel, we could draw a similar example. We can feel very gifted when God's call is so unmistakably focused in its drawing power, for this is the best of times for decisions.

2. Second Time. Quite frequently we experience a time of [176] alternating certainties and doubts, of exhilarating strength and debilitating weakness, of consolation and of desolation. As a matter of fact, this time is very privileged, because the discernment of spirits which is called for is an entrance into understanding a language of God spoken within our very being. We can gain much light and understanding from the experience of consolation and desolation, and so this time, too, is very special for correct decision-making.

3. Third Time. Sometimes, through no fault of our own, nothing seems to be going on. We are placid, having neither the peace of God's consolation nor the desolation of feeling his absence. It is at this time that we can still think quite clearly

[178]   If election is not made in the first or the second time, two ways follow as to this third time for making it.

THE FIRST WAY
TO MAKE A SOUND AND GOOD ELECTION

It contains six Points.

First Point. The first Point is to put before me the thing on which I want to make election, such as an office or benefice, either to take or leave it; or any other thing whatever which falls under an election that can be changed.

[179]   **Second Point.** Second: It is necessary to keep as aim the end for which I am created, which is to praise God our Lord and save my soul, and, this supposed, to find myself indifferent, without any inordinate propensity; so that I be not more inclined or disposed to take the thing proposed than to leave it, nor more to leave it than to take it, but find myself as in the middle of a balance, to follow what I feel to be more for the glory and praise of God our Lord and the salvation of my soul.

[180]   **Third Point.** Third: To ask of God our Lord to be pleased to move my will and put in my soul what I ought to do regarding the thing proposed, so as to promote more His praise and glory; discussing well and faithfully with my intellect, and choosing agreeably to His most holy pleasure and will.

[181]   **Fourth Point.** Fourth: To consider, reckoning up, how many advantages and utilities follow for me from holding the proposed office or benefice for only the praise of God our Lord and the salvation of my soul, and, to consider likewise, on the contrary, the disadvantages and dangers which there are in having it. Doing the same in the second part, that is, looking

and since we can distinguish no movement from God, we would describe this time as one of our own reasoning process.

We should recall our earlier consideration about ends and means (see [169] above), and so the approach is always within the context of a choice leading to a greater service of God and so for our own salvation. The free and peaceful use of our reasoning abilities shows forth the calm logic of this time.

If a choice is not made within circumstances as described in the First or Second Times, then some helpful hints at proceeding during the time of calm rationality are given according to two patterns as follows: [178]

A. First Pattern of Making a Good and Correct Choice:

1. Clearly place before my mind what it is I want to decide about.

2. Try to be like a balance at equilibrium, without leaning to either side. My end is always clearly before me, but I want to be as free toward the object of my choice as I possibly can be. [179]

3. Pray that God our Lord enlighten and move me in the way leading to his praise and glory. Then I should use my understanding to weigh the matter carefully and attempt to come to a decision consonant with my living out God's will in my life. [180]

4. List and weigh the advantages and the disadvantages for me of the various dimensions of my proposed decision. [181]

109

at the advantages and utilities there are in not having it, and likewise, on the contrary, the disadvantages and dangers in not having the same.

[182] **Fifth Point.** Fifth: After I have thus discussed and reckoned up on all sides about the thing proposed, to look where reason more inclines: and so, according to the greater inclination of reason, and not according to any inclination of sense, deliberation should be made on the thing proposed.

[183] **Sixth Point.** Sixth, such election, or deliberation, made, the person who has made it ought to go with much diligence to prayer before God our Lord and offer Him such election, that His Divine Majesty may be pleased to receive and confirm it, if it is to His greater service and praise.

[184]
THE SECOND WAY
TO MAKE A GOOD AND SOUND ELECTION

It contains four Rules and one Note.

First Rule. The first is that that love which moves me and makes me choose such thing should descend from above, from the love of God, so that he who chooses feel first in himself that that love, more or less, which he has for the thing which he chooses, is only for his Creator and Lord.

[185] **Second Rule.** The second, to set before me a man whom I have never seen nor known, and I[1] desiring all his perfection, to consider what I would tell him to do and elect for the greater glory of God our Lord, and the greater perfection of his soul, and I, doing likewise, to keep the rule which I set for the other.

[1] I *is added, perhaps in St. Ignatius' hand.*

5. Consider now which alternative seems more reasonable. [182] Then I will decide according to the more weighty motives and not from my selfish or sensual inclination.

6. Having come to the decision, I now turn to God again [183] and ask him to accept and confirm it if it is for his greater service and glory by bringing it into the ambit of the Second or First Time.

B. Second Pattern of Making a Correct and Good Choice: [184]

1. Since the love of God should motivate my life, I should check myself whether the greater or less attachment for the object of choice is solely because of my Creator and Lord.

2. I present myself with a person whom I have never met [185] before, but who has sought my help in his attempt to respond better to God's call to him. I see what I would tell him, and then I observe the advice which I would so readily give to another for whom I want the best.

[186]   **Third Rule.** The third, to consider, as if I were at the point of death, the form and measure which I would then want to have kept in the way of the present election, and regulating myself by that election, let me make my decision in everything.

[187]   **Fourth Rule.** The fourth, looking and considering how I shall find myself on the Day of Judgment, to think how I would then want to have² deliberated about the present matter, and to take now the rule which I would then wish to have kept, in order that I may then find myself in entire pleasure and joy.

[188]   **Note.** The above-mentioned rules for my eternal salvation and peace having been taken, I will make my election and offering to God our Lord, conformably to the sixth Point of the First Way of making election.

---

² To have *is apparently in St. Ignatius' hand.*

3. If I were at the moment of death and so I would have [186] the freedom and clarity of that time, what would be the decision I would want to have made now? I will guide myself by this insight and make my present decision in conformity with it.

4. I see myself standing before Christ my Judge when this [187] life has ended, and I find myself talking with him about the decision which I have made at this moment in my life. I choose now the course of action which I feel will give me happiness and joy in presenting it to Christ on the day of judgment.

Note: Even after proceeding according to the circumstances [188] outlined above, I will take the decision which I have reached by these approaches and beg God our Lord to accept and confirm it if it is for his greater service and glory by bringing it into the ambit of the Second or First Time.

[189]   TO AMEND AND REFORM ONE'S OWN LIFE
AND STATE

It is to be noted that as to those who are settled in ecclesiastical office or in matrimony — whether they abound much or not in temporal goods — when they have no opportunity or have not a very prompt will to make election about the things which fall under an election that can be changed, it is very helpful, in place of making election, to give them a form and way to amend and reform each his own life and state. That is, putting his creation, life and state for the glory and praise of God our Lord and the salvation of his own soul, to come and arrive at this end, he ought to consider much and ponder through the Exercises and Ways of Election, as has been explained, how large a house and household he ought to keep, how he ought to rule and govern it, how he ought to teach and instruct it by word and by example; likewise of his means, how much he ought to take for his household and house; and how much to dispense to the poor and to other pious objects, not wanting nor seeking any other thing except in all and through all the greater praise and glory of God our Lord.

For let each one think that he will benefit himself in all spiritual things in proportion as he goes out of his self-love, will and interest.

SOME DIRECTIONS FOR THE RENEWAL OF [189]

OR RECOMMITMENT TO A STATE

OR WAY OF LIFE ALREADY CHOSEN

Often in retreat I find myself not so much faced with the question of a new decision, but rather with the living out of a choice already made. This can be as true of the permanent state of life represented in marriage or priesthood as of the more changeable way of life represented in particular jobs or positions.

During the course of the Exercises, it may be quite profitable to take stock of how my living out of a particular means which I have chosen is truly responding to the faithful call of God. The service and love of God and of neighbor should shine out in my dedication. At this time, I should deepen the attitudes and search out the ways which will better enable me to live the Christ-life in my own surroundings and environment. For my progress in living out my life in Christ will be in proportion to the surrender of my own self-love and of my own will and interests.

THIRD WEEK

[190]

THE FIRST CONTEMPLATION

AT MIDNIGHT IS

FIRST
DAY

HOW CHRIST OUR LORD WENT FROM BETHANY TO JERUSALEM TO THE LAST SUPPER INCLUSIVELY

([289]); and it contains the Preparatory Prayer, three Preludes, six Points and one Colloquy.

Prayer. The usual Preparatory Prayer.

[191]

First Prelude. The first Prelude is to bring to memory the narrative; which is here how Christ our Lord sent two Disciples from Bethany to Jerusalem to prepare the Supper, and then He Himself went there with the other Disciples; and how, after having eaten the Paschal Lamb, and having supped, He washed their feet and gave His most Holy Body and Precious Blood to His Disciples, and made them a discourse, after Judas went to sell his Lord.

[192]

Second Prelude. The second, a composition, seeing the place. It will be here to consider the road from Bethany to Jerusalem, whether broad, whether narrow, whether level, etc.; likewise the place of the Supper, whether large, whether small, whether of one kind or whether of another.

[193]

Third Prelude. The third, to ask for what I want. It will be here grief, feeling and confusion because for my sins the Lord is going to the Passion.

[194]

First Point. The first Point is to see the persons of the Supper, and, reflecting

THE THIRD WEEK

The First Day and The First Contemplation: [190]

The Last Supper

PREPARATION: I take time to make the usual preparatory reverence and to petition that God direct everything in my day more and more to his praise and service.

GRACE: The gift I seek from God is his allowing me to enter [193] into a sorrow and shame as I stay with Christ in his sufferings borne on my behalf and because of my sins.

THE SETTING: To enter as fully as I can into the preparations [191, for the Passover Meal and into the whole event we call the Last 192, Supper is my purpose in this contemplation. It goes beyond pic- 194, turing the scene or reading the account in words. I try to listen to the way words are spoken, I attempt to see the expression on 195, the face, I am present with as heightened an awareness as I can 196, muster, so that I enter into the mystery I am contemplating. The 197] Gospel accounts depict the preparations, the Supper itself, Christ's washing of the feet of his Apostles, his giving of his Body and Blood in the Eucharist, and his final words to them.

In addition, during this Third Week, I should make even greater effort to labor with Christ through all his anguish, his struggle, his suffering, or what he desires to suffer. At the time of the Passion, I should pay special attention to how the divinity hides itself so that Jesus seems so utterly human and helpless. To realize that Christ loves me so much that he willingly suffers everything for my rejections and sins makes me ask: What can I, in response, do for him?

on myself, to see to drawing some profit from them.

Second Point. The second, to hear what they are talking about, and likewise to draw some profit from it.

Third Point. The third, to look at what they are doing, and draw some profit.

[195]   **Fourth Point.** The fourth, to consider that which Christ our Lord is suffering in His Humanity,[1] or wants to suffer, according to the passage which is being contemplated, and here to commence with much vehemence and to force myself to grieve, be sad and weep, and so to labor through the other points which follow.

[196]   **Fifth Point.** The fifth, to consider how the Divinity hides Itself, that is, how It could destroy Its enemies and does not do it, and how It leaves the most sacred Humanity to suffer so very cruelly.

[197]   **Sixth Point.** The sixth, to consider how He suffers all this for my sins, etc.; and what I ought to do and suffer for Him.

[198]   **Colloquy.** I will finish with a Colloquy to Christ our Lord, and, at the end, with an OUR FATHER.

[199]   **Note.** It is to be noted, as was explained before and in part, that in the Colloquies I ought to discuss and ask according to the subject matter, that is, according as I find myself tempted or consoled, and according as I desire to have one virtue or another, as I want to dispose of myself in one direction or another, as I want to grieve or rejoice at the thing which I am contemplating; in fine, asking that which I more efficaciously desire as to any particular things. And in this way I can make one Colloquy only, to Christ our Lord, or, if the matter or devotion move me, three Colloquies, one to the Mother, another to the Son, another to the Father, in the same form as was said in

---

[1] In His Humanity *is in St. Ignatius' hand, correcting* the Humanity of *before* Christ.

COLLOQUY: I speak to Jesus, my Lord and Savior, and stay [198] with him through everything that happens. I close the period with an Our Father.

Note: Because of the intimacy involved during the contempla- [199] tions of the Passion, it might be well to review some aspects of the time called "colloquy." Just as in human situations of taking care of the sick or of ministering to the dying, our presence is often more important than our faltering words or awkward actions, so too *to be with* Christ in his Passion describes our prayer response at this time better than any words or actions. Previously we described the colloquy as the intimate conversation between friends. Now we open out that description to include the depth of feeling, love, and compassion, which allows us just *to be there.*

Sometimes, still, we may want to pour out our consolations, our temptations, our fears, our hardness of heart to Christ our Lord. In times of great need, we may find the intensity of our begging reflected in our use of the threefold colloquy. We should remember that faced with the suffering of the Passion

the SECOND WEEK, in the meditation of the THREE PAIRS, with the Note which follows THE PAIRS.

[200]

SECOND CONTEMPLATION
IN THE MORNING
IT WILL BE

SECOND
DAY

FROM THE SUPPER TO THE
GARDEN INCLUSIVELY

Prayer. The usual Preparatory Prayer.

[201]

First Prelude. The first Prelude is the narrative and it will be here how Christ our Lord went down with His eleven Disciples from Mount Sion, where He made the Supper, to the Valley of Josaphat. Leaving the eight in a part of the Valley and the other three in a part of the Garden, and putting Himself in prayer, He sweats sweat as drops of blood,[1] and after He prayed three times to the Father and wakened His three Disciples, and after the enemies at His voice fell down, Judas giving Him the kiss of peace, and St. Peter cutting off the ear of Malchus, and Christ putting it in its place; being taken as a malefactor, they lead Him down the valley, and then up the side, to the house of Annas.

[202]

Second Prelude. The second is to see the place. It will be here to consider the road from Mount Sion to the Valley of Josaphat, and likewise the Garden, whether wide, whether large, whether of one kind, whether of another.

[203]

Third Prelude. The third is to ask for what I want. It belongs to the Passion to ask for grief with Christ in grief, anguish with Christ in anguish, tears and

---

[1] As drops of blood *is in St. Ignatius' hand, replacing* like a bloody sweat.

we may have to pray even for the gift of letting ourselves want to experience it with Christ, according to the manner suggested after the Meditation on the Three Types of Persons, in the Note at [157] above.

The Second Contemplation [200]

The Agony in the Garden

PREPARATION: I take the time to make the usual preparatory reverence and dedication of my day.

GRACE: I continue to pray for the gift of being able to feel sor- [203] row with Christ in sorrow, to be anguished with Christ's anguish, and even to experience tears and deep grief because of all the afflictions which Christ endures for me.

THE SETTING: The Gospels give the details of the event: [201, Christ and his disciples leaving the Upper Room to go towards 202] the garden of Gethsemani. There Jesus takes Peter, James, and John, and goes apart to pray. He experiences such turmoil of spirit that his sweat becomes as drops of blood. Waking his sleepy disciples, he faces the mob, is identified by the kiss of Judas, and is led away to the house of Annas. I labor to enter as fully into the account as I possibly can.

interior pain at such great pain which Christ suffered for me.

[204]   **First Note.** In this second Contemplation, after the Preparatory Prayer is made, with the three Preludes already mentioned, the same form of proceeding will be kept through the Points and Colloquy as was kept in the first Contemplation, on the Supper.

And at the hour of Mass and Vespers two repetitions will be made on the first and second Contemplation, and then, before supper, the senses will be applied on the two above-said Contemplations, always prefixing the Preparatory Prayer and the three Preludes, according to the subject matter, in the same form as was said and explained in the SECOND WEEK.

[205]   **Second Note.** According as age, disposition and physical condition help the person who is exercising himself, he will make each day the five Exercises or fewer.

[206]   **Third Note.** In this THIRD WEEK the second and sixth Additions will in part be changed.

The second will be, immediately on awaking, to set before me where I am going and to what, and summing up a little the contemplation which I want to make, according as the Mystery shall be, to force myself, while I am getting up and dressing, to be sad and grieve over such great grief and such great suffering of Christ our Lord.

The sixth will be changed, so as not to try to bring joyful thoughts, although good and holy, as, for instance, are those on the Resurrection and on heavenly glory, but rather to draw myself to grief and to pain and anguish, bringing to mind frequently the labors, fatigues and pains of Christ our Lord, which He suffered from the moment when He was born up to the Mystery of the Passion in which I find myself at present.

[207]   **Fourth Note.** The Particular Examen on the Exercises and present Additions, will be made as it was made in the past Week.

FURTHER DIRECTIONS [204]

1. The second contemplation, as well as all that follow, is done after the manner of the first contemplation dealing with the Last Supper. During the Third Week, two Scripture passages are given for each day, so that the usual repetitions are made, leading to the Application of the Senses as the final period of prayer.

2. Depending upon the age, the health, and the condition of [205] the retreatant, five exercises a day are encouraged, but fewer may be more desirable because of particular circumstances.

3. In the Third Week, some modifications must again be made [206] in the helps for prayer.

Because of the subject matter of the Passion, I make an effort while rising and dressing to be sad and solemn because of the great sorrow and suffering of Christ our Lord.

Throughout the day, I am careful not to bring up pleasant thoughts, even though they are good and holy, as for example thoughts about the Resurrection and life of glory. Rather I try to maintain a certain attitude of sorrow and anguish by calling to mind frequently the labors, fatigue, and suffering which Christ our Lord endured from the time of his birth down to the particular mystery of the Passion which I am presently contemplating.

In a similar way, the Particular Examen of Conscience should [207] be applied to the exercises and my observation of the helps applicable to this Week, just as it was done in the past Weeks.

[208]   **Second Day.** The second day at midnight, the Contemplation will be from the Garden to the house of Annas inclusive ([291]), and in the morning from the house of Annas to the house of Caiphas inclusive ([292]), and then the two repetitions and the application of the senses, as has been already said.

Third Day. The third day, at midnight, from the house of Caiphas to Pilate, inclusive ([293]); and in the morning, from Pilate to Herod inclusive ([294]); and then the repetitions and senses, in the same form as has been already said.

Fourth Day. The fourth day, at midnight, from Herod to Pilate ([295]), doing and contemplating up to half through the Mysteries of the same house of Pilate, and then, in the Exercise of the morning, the other Mysteries which remained of the same house; and the repetitions and the senses, as has been said.

Fifth Day. The fifth day, at midnight, from the house of Pilate up to the Crucifixion ([296]), and in the morning from His being raised on the Cross until He expired ([297]), then the two repetitions, and the senses.

Sixth Day. The sixth day, at midnight, from the Descent from the Cross to the Tomb, exclusive ([298]) and in the morning from the Tomb, inclusive, to the house where Our Lady was, after her Son was buried.

The Second Day [208]

1. The contemplation on events from the Garden to the house of Annas (see no. 58 at [291] below).

2. The contemplation on events from the house of Annas to the house of Caiaphas (see no. 59 at [292] below). The usual repetitions should be made, with the Application of the Senses being the final prayer period of the day.

The Third Day

1. The contemplation on events from the house of Caiaphas to the house of Pilate (see no. 60 at [293] below).

2. The contemplation on events from the house of Pilate to the palace of Herod (see no. 61 at [294] below). Then the repetitions and Application of the Senses are to be done as noted at [204] above.

The Fourth Day

1. The contemplation on events from Herod's palace back to the house of Pilate (see no. 62 at [295] below).

2. The contemplation on events with Pilate (see no. 62 at [295]). The same procedure should be followed for the repetitions and the Application of the Senses.

The Fifth Day

1. The contemplation on events from the house of Pilate to the crucifixion (see no. 63 at [296] below).

2. The contemplation on events from the raising of the Cross to Jesus' death (see no. 64 at [297] below). The repetitions follow as usual, along with the Application of the Senses.

The Sixth Day

1. The contemplation on events from the taking down from the Cross to the burial (see no. 65 at [298]).

Seventh Day. The seventh day, a Contemplation on the whole Passion together, in the Exercise of midnight and of the morning, and in place of the two repetitions and of the senses one will consider all that day, as frequently as he can, how the most holy Body of Christ our Lord remained separated and apart from the Soul: and where and how It remained buried. Likewise, one will consider the loneliness of Our Lady, whose grief and fatigue were so great: then, on the other side, the loneliness of the Disciples.

[209]

Note. It is to be noted that whoever wants to dwell more on the Passion, has to take in each Contemplation fewer Mysteries; that is to say, in the first Contemplation, the Supper only; in the second, the Washing of the Feet; in the third, the giving of the Blessed Sacrament to them; in the fourth, the discourse which Christ made to them; and so through the other Contemplations and Mysteries.

Likewise, after having finished the Passion, let him take for an entire day the half of the whole Passion, and the second day the other half, and the third day the whole Passion.

On the contrary, whoever would want to shorten more in the Passion, let him take at midnight the Supper, in the morning the Garden, at the hour of Mass the house of Annas, at the hour of Vespers the house of Caiphas, in place of the hour before supper the house of Pilate; so that, not making repetitions, nor the Application of the Senses, he make each day five distinct Exercises, and in each Exercise take a distinct Mystery of Christ our Lord. And after thus finishing the whole Passion, he can, another day, do all the Passion together in one Exercise, or in different ones, as it will seem to him that he will be better able to help himself.

2. The contemplation on events from the burial to Mary's waiting in sorrow.

The repetitions follow as usual, along with the Application of the Senses.

The Seventh Day

1. The contemplation on events of the whole Passion.

2. A repetition on the whole of the Passion. In place of formal prayer periods, I let the effect of Christ's death permeate my being and the world around me for the rest of the day. I consider the desolation of Our Lady, her great sorrow and weariness, and also that of the disciples.

Note: If we want to spend more time on the Passion, the [209] mysteries can be so divided that, for example, only the Supper is considered in one prayer period, then Christ's washing of the feet of his Apostles in another, next the institution of the Eucharist, and finally the farewell discourse of Christ. The other mysteries which make up the total Passion account could be similarly divided up.

After the Passion has been contemplated in its various mysteries over some days, there is the possibility of taking one full day on the first half of the Passion, and a second day on the other half, and a final day reviewing the whole of the Passion.

But if we wish to spend less time on the Passion, we could use a different mystery for each of the prayer periods, eliminating all repetitions and Applications of the Senses. After we have finished contemplating the Passion in this way, we could spend one more day just letting the Passion in its whole sweep pervade our day. In all these suggested approaches, the good progress of the retreat is always the guiding consideration.

RULES

TO PUT ONESELF IN ORDER FOR THE FUTURE
AS TO EATING

First Rule. The first rule is that it is well to abstain less from bread, because it is not a food as to which the appetite is used to act so inordinately, or to which temptation urges as in the case of the other foods.

[211] **Second Rule.** The second: Abstinence appears more convenient as to drinking, than as to eating bread. So, one ought to look much what is helpful to him, in order to admit it, and what does him harm, in order to discard it.

[212] **Third Rule.** The third: As to foods, one ought to have the greatest and most entire abstinence, because as the appetite is more ready to act inordinately, so temptation is more ready in making trial, on this head. And so abstinence in foods, to avoid disorder, can be kept in two ways, one by accustoming oneself to eat coarse foods; the other, if one takes delicate foods, by taking them in small quantity.

[213] **Fourth Rule.** The fourth: Guarding against falling into sickness, the more a man leaves off from what is suitable, the more quickly he will reach the mean which he ought to keep in his eating and drinking; for two reasons: the first, because by so helping and disposing himself, he will many times experience more the interior knowledge, consolations and Divine inspirations to show him the mean which is proper for him; the second, because if the person sees himself in such abstinence not with so great corporal strength or disposition for the Spiritual Exercises, he will easily come to judge what is more suitable to his bodily support.

[214] **Fifth Rule.** The fifth: While the person is eating, let him consider as if he saw Christ our Lord eating with His Apostles, and how He drinks and how He looks and how He speaks; and let him see to imitating Him. So that

GUIDELINES WITH REGARD TO EATING [210]

Preliminary Note: As I begin to grow in my knowledge of Jesus Christ and union with him through the exercises of the Second and Third Weeks, it is clear that the "sense of Christ" is meant to permeate my whole being and all my activities. To reflect on the daily and commonplace activity of eating is to emphasize how total is my response to follow Jesus Christ. As St. Paul says, "whether you eat or drink—whatever you do—you should do all for the glory of God" (1 Cor. 10:31).

The following guidelines, then, are meant to model a reflective approach about my conduct in every part of my life so that being ever more fully penetrated by the life of Christ within me, I show forth a proper ordering of the various areas of my life. In the words of St. Paul, "whatever you do, work at it with your whole being" (Col. 3:23). Through such guidelines, I can begin even now to live out the reordering process which has begun to be effected in me during the course of the retreat. I also look forward to the time after the retreat when these guidelines are meant to be an integral part of my life.

A. *General Principle*

1. It is while I am eating that I should reflect upon Christ and [214] his apostles at table. I should try to enter into the presence of Christ so fully that I have a sense of how Jesus eats and drinks, how he speaks and handles himself in the context of a meal. Even at the very time of doing this exercise of the imagination, I will find that I no longer have the food itself as a focus of my attention. As a result, I will come to a greater order in my own conduct at table, perhaps both in what I eat and in how I act while eating.

B. *Particular Applications*

2. There seems to be less problem for a proper ordering in [210] my life when it is a matter of bread or the ordinary staples of diet.

3. There does seem to be a greater care necessary when I con- [211] sider the area of drink. Whatever the beverage—beer, soda, coffee, milk, wine, and so on—I should consider what is helpful and so pursue the proper moderation for myself, and also what may be harmful and so avoid the disordered excess.

the principal part of the intellect shall occupy itself in the consideration of Christ our Lord, and the lesser part in the support of the body; because in this way he will get greater system and order as to how he ought to behave and manage himself.

[215]   **Sixth Rule.** The sixth: Another time, while he is eating, he can take another consideration, either on the life of Saints, or on some pious Contemplation, or on some spiritual affair which he has to do, because, being intent on such thing, he will take less delight and feeling in the corporal food.

[216]   **Seventh Rule.** The seventh: Above all, let him guard against all his soul being intent on what he is eating, and in eating let him not go hurriedly, through appetite, but be master of himself, as well in the manner of eating as in the quantity which he eats.

[217]   **Eighth Rule.** The eighth: To avoid disorder, it is very helpful, after dinner or after supper, or at another hour when one feels no appetite for eating, to decide with oneself for the coming dinner or supper, and so on, each day, the quantity which it is suitable that he should eat. Beyond this let him not go because of any appetite or temptation, but rather, in order to conquer more all inordinate appetite and temptation of the enemy, if he is tempted to eat more, let him eat less.

4. When I consider the wide variety of food available to me, [212] I should be more conscious of its appeal to my appetites and so of the necessity for a greater sense of control. To avoid disorder concerning foods, a certain abstinence can be practiced in two ways:

   (a) by seeking out less delicate foods, even to a greater dependence on the staples within the diet;
   (b) by eating sparingly of rich and delicate foods.

5. It is good to discover a proper mean for myself in my eating [213] habits. While taking care not to fall sick, I can reduce my intake of food in order to come to such a mean. There are two reasons why seeking such a mean can be profitable:

   (a) commonly the observation of a mean in my diet provides a disposition whereby I will often experience more abundant lights, consolations, and divine movements within my spirit. These experiences, in turn, may confirm me in the ordering of such a mean in eating;
   (b) when I discover that observing a certain chosen mean in diet brings about an inability to continue well in the performance of the exercises of the retreat, I will then come more easily to adjust such a mean in order that I can have the necessary strength and health for my ordinary daily life and activity.

C. *Particular Attitudes*

6. In regard to my attention at a meal time, I may find a read- [215] ing about a saint or a particular spiritual apostolate very helpful in fixing my focus beyond the mere gratification of my hunger. Music, too, can provide a reflective and relaxed setting for meals.

7. If the whole focus of my attention at meals is upon food [216] itself, I can find that I am carried away by my appetites. I may also discover that I am bolting my food so hurriedly that there is little evidence of a Christ-behavior in my activity of eating a meal. Both in the amount of food eaten and in the way it is eaten, I should be ordering my life in Christ.

8. If I were to plan ahead for my meals, I may find that an [217] order in my eating habits is far easier to accomplish. For example, it can be very helpful after lunch or after dinner or at a time when I do not feel a desire for food to determine how much I will eat at the next meal. Then at the time of the meal itself, I should not exceed that amount which I set myself, no matter how strong the temptation might be. In fact, if I find myself strongly moved by my appetites to eat more, I should take even less than the amount I had predetermined.

FOURTH WEEK

[218]

THE FIRST CONTEMPLATION

HOW CHRIST OUR LORD APPEARED TO OUR LADY

([299]); **Prayer.** The usual Preparatory Prayer.

[219]   **First Prelude.** The first Prelude is the narrative, which is here how, after Christ expired on the Cross, and the Body, always united with the Divinity, remained separated from the Soul, the blessed Soul, likewise united with the Divinity, went down to Hell, and taking from there the just souls, and coming to the Sepulchre and being risen, He appeared to His Blessed Mother in Body and in Soul.

[220]   **Second Prelude.** The second, a composition, seeing the place; which will be here to see the arrangement of the Holy Sepulchre and the place or house of Our Lady, looking at its parts in particular; likewise the room, the oratory, etc.

[221]   **Third Prelude.** The third, to ask for what I want, and it will be here to ask for grace to rejoice and be glad intensely at so great glory and joy of Christ our Lord.

[222]   **First Point, Second Point, and Third Point.** Let the first, second and third Points be the same usual ones which we took in the Supper of Christ our Lord.

[223]   **Fourth Point.** The fourth, to consider how the Divinity, which seemed to hide Itself in the Passion, now appears and shows Itself so marvellously in the most holy Resurrection by Its true and most holy effects.

THE FOURTH WEEK

The First Day and the First Contemplation: [218]

the Appearance of Christ our Lord to Mary

PREPARATION: I take the time for the usual preparatory reverence and petition that God direct everything in my day more and more to his praise and service.

GRACE: I beg for the gift of being able to enter into the joy [221]
and consolation of Jesus in the victory of his risen life.

THE SETTING: In the usual way, I try to enter into this contemplation as fully as I can. Although I do not have a Scripture account to guide my thoughts, I can easily know the excitement of Jesus in wanting to share the joy of his resurrection with his Mother who had stood by him throughout the Passion. I let the delight and the love of this encounter permeate my being.

[219,
220,
222,
223,
224]

In contrast to the Passion, I should note how much the divinity shines through the person of Christ in all his appearances. The peace and the joy which he wants to share with me can only

[224]   **Fifth Point.** The fifth is to consider the office of consoling which Christ our Lord bears, and to compare how friends are accustomed to console friends.

[225]   **Colloquy.** I will finish with a Colloquy, or Colloquies, according to the subject matter, and an OUR FATHER.

[226]   **First Note.** In the following Contemplations let one go on through all the Mysteries of the Resurrection, in the manner which follows below, up to the Ascension inclusive, taking and keeping in the rest the same form and manner in all the Week of the Resurrection which was taken in all the Week of the Passion. So that, for this first Contemplation, on the Resurrection, let one guide himself as to the Preludes according to the subject matter; and as to the five Points, let them be the same; and let the Additions which are below be the same; and so in all which remains, he can guide himself by the method of the Week of the Passion, as in repetitions, the five Senses, in shortening or lengthening the Mysteries.

[227]   **Second Note.** The second note: Commonly in this FOURTH WEEK, it is more suitable than in the other three past to make four Exercises, and not five: the first, immediately on rising in the morning; the second, at the hour of Mass, or before dinner, in place of the first repetition; the third, at the hour of Vespers, in place of the second repetition; the fourth, before supper, bringing the five Senses on the three Exercises of the same day, noting and lingering on the more principal parts, and where one has felt greater spiritual movements and relish.

[228]   **Third Note.** The third: Though in all the Contemplations so many Points were given in certain number — as three, or five, etc., — the person who is contemplating can set more or fewer Points, according as he finds it better for him. For which it is very helpful, before entering on the Contemplation, to conjecture and mark in certain number the Points which he is to take.

be a gift of God. To realize that the role of consoler which Christ performs in each of his resurrection appearances is the same role he performs now in my life is a faith insight into why I can live my life in a true Christian optimism.

COLLOQUY: According to the circumstances of the setting, I let my response be directed to one or more persons or let it be in the threefold manner to Mary, Christ, and the Father. In every case, I always close the prayer period with an Our Father. [225]

FURTHER DIRECTIONS

1. In all the contemplations of this Fourth Week—the mysteries of the Resurrection through the Ascension inclusive, the usual procedure should be followed as was done in the previous Week. A shortening or lengthening of the Week can easily be made by a selection or division of the various mysteries. The freedom shown in the Week on the Passion should be the guide. [226]

2. Ordinarily it is more in keeping with the atmosphere of relaxed consolation in this Week to have no more than four periods of prayer within the day, although there could be three passages of Scripture presented for contemplation. As a result, the pattern of prayer periods begins with the one upon arising in the morning, the second later in the morning, the third sometime in the afternoon, and the fourth period, which is usually described as the Application of the Senses, in the evening. [227]

This fourth period of prayer centers on those aspects of the preceding three contemplations where the retreatant was more moved and there was greater spiritual relish.

3. As I allow the Scripture passage to present me with the setting for prayer, I know that certain elements provide me with a focus. I should be sure to let these focal points direct my attention during the prayer period so that the general good feeling of this Week with its possible distractions or scattering of attention does not mitigate my response to the Lord. [228]

[229]

Fourth Note. In this FOURTH WEEK, in all the ten Additions the second, the sixth, the seventh and the tenth are to be changed.

The second will be, immediately on awaking, to put before me the Contemplation which I have to make, wanting to arouse feeling and be glad at the great joy and gladness of Christ our Lord.

The sixth, to bring to memory and think of things that move to spiritual pleasure, gladness and joy, as of heavenly glory.

The seventh, to use light or temporal comforts — as, in summer, the coolness; and in winter, the sun or heat — as far as the soul thinks or conjectures that it can help it to be joyful in its Creator and Redeemer.

The tenth: in place of penance, let one regard temperance and all moderation; except it is question of precepts of fasting or of abstinence which the Church commands; because those are always to be fulfilled, if there is no just impediment.

4. In the Fourth Week, I make some modifications in the helps [229] toward making the whole day consistently prayerful.

As soon as I awake, I recall the atmosphere of joy which pervades this Week and review the particular mystery about which I am to contemplate.

Throughout the day, I try to keep myself in a mood which is marked by happiness and spiritual joy. As a result, anything in my environment—the sun and warm weather or the white cover of snow, all the different beauties of nature, and so on—is used to reinforce the atmosphere of consolation.

Obviously, during this period, penance is not in keeping with the total movement, and so only the usual temperance and moderation in all things is encouraged.

[230]   *CONTEMPLATION TO GAIN LOVE*

Note. First, it is well to remark two things:
the first is that love ought to be put more in
deeds than in words.

[231] The second, love consists in interchange
between the two parties; that is to say in the
lover's giving and communicating to the beloved what he has or out of what he has or
can; and so, on the contrary, the beloved to
the lover. So that if the one has knowledge,
he give to the one who has it not. The same
of honors, of riches; and so the one to the
other.

Prayer. The usual Prayer.

[232] **First Prelude.** The first Prelude is a
composition, which is here to see how I
am standing before God our Lord, and of
the Angels and of the Saints interceding
for me.

[233] **Second Prelude.** The second, to ask
for what I want. It will be here to ask
for interior knowledge of so great good
received, in order that being entirely
grateful, I may be able in all to love and
serve His Divine Majesty.

[234] **First Point.** The First Point is, to bring
to memory the benefits received, of Creation, Redemption and particular gifts,
pondering with much feeling how much
God our Lord has done for me, and how
much He has given me of what He has,
and then the same Lord desires to give
me Himself as much as He can, according
to His Divine ordination.

CONTEMPLATION ON THE LOVE OF GOD [230]

Preliminary Note: Before this exercise is presented, two observations should be made:

(1) the first is that love ought to show itself in deeds over and above words;

(2) the second is that love consists in a mutual sharing of [231] goods. For example, a lover gives and shares with the beloved something of his personal gifts or some possession which he has or is able to give; so, too, the beloved shares with the lover. In this way, one who has knowledge shares it with one who does not, and this is true for honors, riches, and so on. In love, one always wants to give to the other.

PREPARATION: I take the usual time to place myself reverently in the presence of my Lord and my God, and beg that God will direct everything in my day more and more to his praise and service.

At this time, I may find it especially helpful to imagine myself [232] standing before God and all his saints who are praying for me.

GRACE: I beg for the gift of an intimate knowledge of all the [233] sharing of goods which God does in his love for me. Filled with gratitude, I want to be empowered to respond just as totally in my love and service of him.

THE SETTING: There are four different focal points which present the subject matter for my prayer:

1. God's gifts to me. [234]

God creates me out of love which desires nothing more than a return of love on my part. So much does he love me that even though I take myself away from him, he continues to be my Savior and Redeemer.

And with this to reflect on myself, considering with much reason and justice, what I ought on my side to offer and give to His Divine Majesty, that is to say, everything that is mine, and myself with it, as one who makes an offering with much feeling:

Take, Lord, and receive all my liberty, my memory, my intellect, and all my will — all that I have and possess. Thou gavest it to me: to Thee, Lord, I return it! All is Thine, dispose of it according to all Thy will. Give me Thy love and grace, for this is enough for me.

[235]

Second Point. The second, to look how God dwells in creatures, in the elements, giving them being, in the plants vegetating, in the animals feeling in them, in men giving them to understand: [1] and so in me, giving me being, animating me, giving me sensation and making me to understand; [2] likewise making a temple of me, being created to the likeness and image of His Divine Majesty; reflecting as much on myself in the way which is said in the first Point, or in another which I feel to be better. In the same manner will be done on each Point which follows.

[236]

Third Point. The third, to consider how God works and labors for me in all things created on the face of the earth — that is, behaves like one who labors — as in the heavens, elements, plants, fruits, cattle, etc., giving them being, preserving them, giving them vegetation and sensation, etc.

Then to reflect on myself.

---

[1] Giving them to understand *is an addition, very probably in St. Ignatius' hand.*

[2] Making me to understand; likewise *is in the Saint's handwriting, correcting a word erased, probably* understanding.

All my natural abilities and gifts, along with the gifts of Baptism and the Eucharist and the special graces lavished upon me, are only so many signs of how much God our Lord shares his life with me. My consolation: who I am by the grace of God!

If I were to respond as a reasonable person, what could I give in return to such a Lover? Moved by love, I may want to express my own love-response in the following words:

TAKE AND RECEIVE

Take, Lord, and receive all my liberty, my memory, my understanding, and my entire will—all that I have and call my own. You have given it all to me. To you, Lord, I return it. Everything is yours; do with it what you will. Give me only your love and your grace. That is enough for me.

2. God's gift of himself to me.   [235]

God not only gives gifts to me, but he literally gives himself to me. His is not only the Word in whom all things are created, but also the Word who becomes flesh and dwells with us. He gives himself to me so that his Body and Blood become the food and drink of my life. He pours out upon me his Spirit so that I can cry out "Abba." God loves me so much that I literally become a dwelling-place or a temple of God—growing in an ever deepening realization of the image and likeness of God which remains the glory of the creation of man and woman.

If I were to make only a reasonable response, what could I do? Moved by love, I may find that I can respond best in words like the TAKE AND RECEIVE.

3. God's labors for me.   [236]

God loves me so much that he enters into the very struggle of life. Like a potter with clay, like a mother in childbirth, or like a mighty force blowing life into dead bones, God labors to share his life and his love. His labors take him even to death on a cross in order to bring forth the life of the Resurrection.

Once more I question myself how I can make a response. Let me look again to the expression of the TAKE AND RECEIVE.

[237] **Fourth Point.** The fourth, to look how all the good things and gifts descend from above, as my poor power from the supreme and infinite power from above; and so justice, goodness, pity, mercy, etc.; as from the sun descend the rays, from the fountain the waters, etc.

Then to finish reflecting on myself, as has been said.

I will end with a Colloquy and an OUR FATHER.

4. God as Giver and Gift.   [237]

God's love shines down upon me like the light rays from the sun, or his love is poured forth lavishly like a fountain spilling forth its waters into an unending stream. Just as I see the sun in its rays and the fountain in its waters, so God pours forth himself in all the gifts which he showers upon me. His delight and his joy is to be with the sons of men—to be with me. He cannot do enough to speak out his love for me—ever calling me to a fuller and better life.

What can I respond to such a generous Giver? Let me consider once again the expression of the TAKE AND RECEIVE.

I close the prayer with an Our Father.

Note: There are a number of approaches which we can use as we pray this Contemplation on the Love of God.

The Contemplation could provide the prayer material for the final day or days of the Fourth Week and so close out the retreat. All four points of the Contemplation could be used in a single prayer period. Then the repetitions would continue to simplify the response throughout the prayer periods of the day. Perhaps one or two points of the Contemplation might provide the material for the whole day, with the usual repetitions being employed.

Another approach would be to use the Contemplation as a whole or with any one of its points as the final prayer period of each day within the Fourth Week, taking the place of the usual Application of the Senses. Perhaps one final day would be spent upon the total material of the Contemplation, after the manner of reviewing the whole of the Passion in the Third Week.

Whatever is more conducive to the good closure of the retreat for the particular retreatant is the determining guide for how to proceed.

[238]

THREE METHODS OF PRAYER
AND FIRST ON THE COMMANDMENTS

FIRST METHOD

The first Method of Prayer is on the Ten Commandments, and on the Seven Deadly Sins, on the Three Powers of the Soul and on the Five Bodily Senses. This method of prayer is meant more to give form, method and exercises, how the soul may prepare itself and benefit in them, and that the prayer may be acceptable, rather than to give any form or way of praying.

I. The Ten Commandments

[239]

First let the equivalent of the second Addition of the SECOND WEEK be made; that is, before entering on the prayer, let the spirit rest a little, the person being seated or walking about, as may seem best to him, considering where he is going and to what. And this same addition will be made at the beginning of all Methods of Prayer.

[240]

Prayer. A Preparatory Prayer, as, for example, to ask grace of God our Lord that I may be able to know in what I have failed as to the Ten Commandments; and likewise to beg grace and help to amend in future, asking for perfect understanding of them, to keep them better and for the greater glory and praise of His Divine Majesty.

[241]

For the first Method of Prayer, it is well to consider and think on the First Commandment, how I have kept it and in what I have failed, keeping to the rule of spending the space of time one says

THREE METHODS OF PRAYING   [238]

Preliminary Note. St. Ignatius of Loyola was anxious to help people to continue to develop their prayer lives. He outlines briefly some ways of praying which we can use when we have no text of Scripture at hand, when we are tired or travelling, or when in general we are left to our own resources. Although there are many far more developed treatises on prayer, Ignatius' simple directives can still be helpful to us today.

A. THE FIRST METHOD OF PRAYING

The first method of praying deals with the matter of the ten commandments, or the seven deadly sins, or the three powers of the soul, or the five senses of the body. What will be described is the preparation for the time of prayer and the ways of moving into the consideration of the matter. The actual praying we will not attempt to formulate.

I. *On the Ten Commandments*

PREPARATION: Before entering into the time for praying, we   [239]
spend some time relaxing, either by sitting or by walking. It is good to take this time to recall what we are about to do. To make this preparation time is important for entering well into all methods of praying.

GRACE: Next we speak out our need for a particular grace from   [240]
God our Lord: begging that we may know how we have failed in keeping the ten commandments, that we might be able to come to a better understanding of them, and that we might be more capable of living them out, to the greater glory and praise of God.

THE METHOD: In order to enter into the first method of pray-   [241]
ing, it is good to reflect upon how we have been faithful and how we have failed in our observance of the first commandment. In the brief time that we center our attention on the first com-

145

the OUR FATHER and the HAIL MARY three times; and if in this time I find faults of mine, to ask pardon and forgiveness for them, and say an OUR FATHER. Let this same method be followed on each one of the Ten Commandments.

[242] **First Note.** It is to be noted that when one comes to think on a Commandment on which he finds he has no habit of sinning, it is not necessary for him to delay so much time, but according as one finds in himself that he stumbles more or less on that Commandment so he ought to keep himself more or less on the consideration and examination of it. And the same is to be observed on the Deadly Sins.

[243] **Second Note.** After having finished the discussion already mentioned on all the Commandments, accusing myself on them and asking grace and help to amend hereafter, I am to finish with a Colloquy to God our Lord, according to the subject matter.

[244] *II. On Deadly Sins*

About the Seven Deadly Sins, after the Addition, let the Preparatory Prayer be made in the way already mentioned, only with the difference that the matter here is of sins that have to be avoided, and before of Commandments that have to be kept: and likewise let the order and rule already mentioned be kept, and the Colloquy.

[245] In order to know better the faults committed in the Deadly Sins, let their contraries be looked at: and so, to avoid them better, let the person purpose and with holy exercises see to acquiring and keeping the seven virtues contrary to them.

mandment, we may become aware of our failings and so we ask pardon and forgiveness of them from God. Before moving on to the next commandment, we will say an Our Father. And so in this same way, we take up each commandment for consideration and for prayer.

Note 1. If we find that we have no failings in regard to a particular commandment, we will move on more quickly to the next one to be considered. But if we find that a particular commandment is very central to our Christian living, we may need to spend more time in consideration. This way of proceeding remains helpful when we take up the matter of the deadly sins. [242]

Note 2. When we have finished our reflections upon all the commandments, both in asking forgiveness and in begging the grace to respond better in the future, we spend the time speaking intimately with God our Lord and saying whatever comes to our mind and from our heart in regard to the particular matter which we have considered in our prayer. [243]

II. *On the Deadly Sins:* (pride, anger, envy, lust gluttony, avarice, sloth) [244]

THE METHOD: The second area which provides matter for this method of praying is a consideration of the deadly sins. We should proceed in the same way as we did in regard to the matter of the commandments. After an initial relaxation time and preparatory prayer for the grace which we are seeking, we move into the consideration of the deadly sins. In contrast with the commandments which are to be faithfully observed, we are now reflecting upon sins or patterns of behavior which are to be avoided. But otherwise our way of proceeding remains the same, with a short time spent in reflecting on each sin, asking forgiveness for failures, saying an Our Father, and so passing through all the sins until we have our final time of intimate prayer with God our Lord.

Note: In order to enter more deeply into the consideration of the seven deadly sins, we should also review the seven virtues which are their contraries. We should pray to grow in these virtues and observe them ever more faithfully. [245]

[246]

III. On the Powers of the Soul

Way. On the three powers of the soul let the same order and rule be kept as on the Commandments, making its Addition, Preparatory Prayer and Colloquy.

[247]

IV. On the Bodily Senses

Way. About the five bodily senses the same order always will be kept, but changing their matter.

[248]

Note. Whoever wants to imitate Christ our Lord in the use of his senses, let him in the Preparatory Prayer recommend himself to His Divine Majesty, and after considering on each sense, say a HAIL MARY or an OUR FATHER.

And whoever wants to imitate Our Lady in the use of the senses, let him in the Preparatory Prayer recommend himself to her, that she may get him grace from Her Son and Lord for it; and after considering on each sense, say a HAIL MARY.

[249]

SECOND METHOD OF PRAYER

It is by contemplating the meaning of each word of the Prayer.

[250]

Addition. The same Addition which was in the First Method of Prayer will be in this second.

[251]

Prayer. The Preparatory Prayer will be made according to the person to whom the prayer is addressed.

[252]

Second Method of Prayer. The Second Method of Prayer is that the person, kneeling or seated, according to the greater disposition in which he finds himself and

III. *On the Three Powers of the Soul* [246]
   (memory, understanding, will)

THE METHOD: A third area which may be proposed as matter
for this method of praying is a consideration of the three powers
of the soul. Once again the same procedure is followed: a short
time for relaxation and recollection, then a preparatory prayer
for the grace which we are seeking, the consideration of the matter itself with its time of begging, thanking, praising, or asking
forgiveness, and a closing out of the period of prayer with a final
intimate speaking to the Lord.

IV. *On the Five Senses of the Body* [247]

THE METHOD: A fourth area which may be proposed as matter for this method of praying is a consideration of the five bodily
senses. The way of proceeding in the prayer period remains the
same, with only the change in the matter being considered.

   Note: Because we may want to imitate Christ our Lord in the [248]
use of our senses, we might begin by placing ourselves humbly
before God our Lord in our preparation time. As we consider
each sense, we say either one Hail Mary or one Our Father. We
may wish, however, to pray to imitate Our Lady in the use of
our senses. In our preparation time, we place ourselves before
her and beg that she may obtain for us this very grace from her
Son and Lord, Then after we consider each sense, we say one
Hail Mary.

   B. THE SECOND METHOD OF PRAYING [249]

   The second method of praying centers upon contemplating
the meaning of each word in a traditional prayer formula.

PREPARATION: We always observe the time interval in which [250]
we relax and reflect upon what we are about to do.

GRACE: The preparatory prayer in which we beg for a par- [251]
ticular grace is addressed to the person who is the subject of the
traditional prayer which we are considering.

THE METHOD: We can understand the second method of [252]
praying in the following way. We use the Our Father as our ex-

as more devotion accompanies him, keeping the eyes closed or fixed on one place, without going wandering with them, says FATHER, and is on the consideration of this word as long as he finds meanings, comparisons, relish and consolation in considerations pertaining to such word. And let him do in the same way on each word of the OUR FATHER, or of any other prayer which he wants to say in this way.

[253] **First Rule.** The first Rule is that he will be an hour on the whole OUR FATHER in the manner already mentioned. Which finished, he will say a HAIL MARY, CREED, SOUL OF CHRIST, and HAIL, HOLY QUEEN, vocally or mentally, according to the usual way.

[254] **Second Rule.** The Second Rule is that, should the person who is contemplating the OUR FATHER find in one word, or in two, matter so good to think over, and relish and consolation, let him not care to pass on, although the hour ends on what he finds. The hour finished, he will say the rest of the OUR FATHER in the usual way.

[255] **Third Rule.** The third is that if on one word or two of the OUR FATHER one has lingered for a whole hour, when he will want to come back another day to the prayer, let him say the above-mentioned word, or the two, as he is accustomed; and on the word which immediately follows let him commence to contemplate, according as was said in the second Rule.

[256] **First Note.** It is to be noted that, the OUR FATHER finished, in one or in many days, the same has to be done with the HAIL MARY and then with the other prayers, so that for some time one is always exercising himself in one of them.

[257] **Second Note.** The second note is that, the prayer finished, turning, in few words, to the person to whom he has prayed, let him ask for the virtues or graces of which he feels he has most need.

ample. Our position during such prayer can be kneeling or sitting, whichever seems to be more conducive to praying and better fitted to our own devotion. We take care to keep our attention focused in this method of praying by taking advantage of a help like keeping our eyes closed or fixing our gaze upon some one place or object. As we begin our consideration, we say "Father," and we let this word remain within us for so long a time as we find meanings, comparisons, relish, and consolation coming from our reflection upon this word. We act in a similar way with every word of the Our Father or of any prayer we may want to pray in this method.

Rule 1. We fill out our time for prayer by reflecting on each word of a prayer we have chosen, and then we close out the time by saying the Hail Mary, the Creed, the Soul of Christ, and the Hail Holy Queen, aloud or not, in the usual way. [253]

Rule 2. We observe that when one word or two of the prayer, Our Father, occupies our full attention with relish and consolation, we do not hurry on. Rather we remain where we find devotion even though the full time for praying elapses in this way. When we have come to the end of our prayer period, we simply pray the rest of the Our Father in the usual way. [254]

Rule 3. We may spend a whole hour of prayer on one word or two of the Our Father. If we wish to continue using this method of praying on successive days, we can then say the words which we have previously prayed over in the usual way, and on the next word which follows we can once more begin to contemplate according to this second method. [255]

Note 1: We may spend some days in praying the Our Father according to this second method. We could then use the Hail Mary, and continue on with other traditional prayers so that this method of praying can remain a helpful pattern for our life of prayer. [256]

Note 2: When this second method of praying is used, we bring the time of prayer to completion by turning to the person to whom we have addressed our petition for grace, and in a brief manner plead now the more fervently for the virtues or graces which we feel that we most need. [257]

[258]   THIRD METHOD OF PRAYER

It will be by rhythm.

Addition. The Addition will be the same as in the First and Second Methods of Prayer.

Prayer. The Preparatory Prayer will be as in the Second Method of Prayer.

Third Method of Prayer. The Third Method of Prayer is that with each breath in or out, one has to pray mentally, saying one word of the OUR FATHER, or of another prayer which is being recited: so that only one word be said between one breath and another, and while the time from one breath to another lasts, let attention be given chiefly to the meaning of such word, or to the person to whom he recites it, or to his own baseness, or to the difference from such great height to his own so great lowness. And in the same form and rule he will proceed on the other words of the OUR FATHER; and the other prayers, that is to say, the HAIL MARY, the SOUL OF CHRIST, the CREED, and the HAIL, HOLY QUEEN, he will make as he is accustomed.

[259]   **First Rule.** The First Rule is, on the other day, or at another hour, that he wants to pray, let him say the HAIL MARY in rhythm, and the other prayers as he is accustomed; and so on, going through the others.

[260]   **Second Rule.** The second is that whoever wants to dwell more on the prayer by rhythm, can say all the above-mentioned prayers or part of them, keeping the same order of the breath by rhythm, as has been explained.

C. THE THIRD METHOD OF PRAYING [258]

The third method of praying consists in our making use of a certain rhythmical flow.

PREPARATION: We take the usual time to relax and reflect upon what we are about to do.

GRACE: We make the preparatory prayer in which we beg for a particular grace by addressing the person ·who is the subject of the particular vocal prayer which we are using.

THE METHOD: The third method of praying can be described in the following way. We are so relaxed that our breathing in and out comes at a slow but steady pace. If we use the Our Father, we say one word at a time while we breathe in and out. And so with the next breath, we say or take up the next word. In the interval of time which takes place in our breathing in and out, we look mainly to the meaning of the word, or to the person whom we are addressing, or to our own neediness, or to the difference between the holiness of God and his saints and our own sinfulness. In this way, we proceed word by word through the Our Father. To fill out the time set aside for our prayer, we could then say other prayers in our ordinary way—prayers such as the Hail Mary, Soul of Christ, the Creed, and the Hail Holy Queen.

Rule 1. If on another day or at another time in the same day [259] we want to pray more according to this third method, we can then use the Hail Mary. Again we proceed word by word in the same rhythmical flow of breathing. All the traditional vocal prayers of the Church are available for us to use in this way.

Rule 2. If we find that we have the time and that we work [260] well with this third method of praying, we can use one prayer and, upon completing it, move on to another and so proceed throughout the whole prayer period, always keeping the same rhythmical flow of breathing for each one of the prayers which we consider.

SCRIPTURE TEXTS

FOR

THE FOUNDATION: FACT AND PRACTICE

Preliminary Note: Although St. Ignatius of Loyola did not suggest any Scripture texts during the time for considering The Foundation, or even during the meditations of the First Week, it is a common practice to approach or reinforce this material through the use of Scripture.

Some suggested texts are presented for this early part of the Exercises in a manner that is consistent with the Ignatian presentation for the Second, Third, and Fourth Weeks. The texts presented are to be used or not, always in view of the needs of a particular retreatant and the abilities of an individual retreat director. Different texts, as well as additional texts, are possible because the only criterion is always the good progress of this particular retreatant.

In the Second, Third, and Fourth Weeks, the Scripture texts given below are those suggested by St. Ignatius himself.

A. Some suggested Scripture Texts for the Foundation:

1. MAN IS CREATED

Psalm 103

Focus: how good God is to mankind

Note: When praying a psalm, a number of approaches can be used:
(1) very slowly reading through the psalm, making it one's prayer expression; or
(2) letting certain lines or phrases hold one's attention for the whole period of prayer; or
(3) thoughtfully reading through the psalm a number of times within the prayer period.

2. GOD THE CREATOR
Psalm 104
Focus: how great God is.

3. THE LORD, OUR GOD
>> Psalm 105
>> Focus: how faithful God is to mankind.

4. GRATITUDE TO GOD
>> Psalm 136
>> Focus: the mantra-like response is made to every thought about God—"For his mercy endures forever."

5. THE CREATION OF MAN
>> Genesis 1-2:4
>> Focus: a good creation has men and women at its center.

6. THE WORD IN CREATION
>> John 1:1-14
>> Focus: God's Word is the center and source of all life.

7. THE NEARNESS OF GOD
>> Psalm 139
>> Focus: how well God knows me and how close he is to me.

8. GOD INVITES US
>> Isaiah 55
>> Focus: God gives so freely and so effectively.

9. GOD'S DWELLING AMONG MEN
>> Revelation 21:1-8
>> Focus: God is always with us in this "new earth."

10. CHRIST AS SOURCE OF ALL LIFE
>> Colossians 1:15-23
>> Focus: Jesus Christ is the center of creation and our center.

11. WE MUST BE FREE TO RESPOND
    Genesis 12:1-9 and Genesis 22:1-18
    Focus: Abraham has faith in God's lead.

12. WE MUST BE FREE TO RESPOND
    Acts 9:1-19
    Focus: Saul surrenders to Christ's lead.

13. WE MUST BE FREE TO RESPOND
    Mark 10:17-31
    Focus: the following of God's call is free, but costly.

B. Some Suggested Scripture Texts for the First Week:

14. THE FIRST SIN OF MAN
    Genesis 3:1-19
    Focus: how devastating is one sin and its effect.

15. THE HISTORY OF SIN
    Psalm 106
    Focus: how many times men continue to reject a loving God.

16. REJECTION OF GOD AS REJECTION OF LIFE
    Matthew 13:4-23
    Focus: God's seed within us must be nurtured or else death results.

17. RECOGNITION OF SIN
    2 Samuel 12:1-15
    Focus: how blind a man can be to his own action.

18. EXPERIENCE OF SIN
    Romans 7:13-23
    Focus: how deep the effects of sin are in us.

19. PERSONAL RESPONSIBILITY FOR SIN
    Ezekiel 18:1-32
    Focus: "I" am responsible for my choices.

20. SIN CONFESSED BEFORE GOD
    Isaiah 59:1-21
    Focus: as sinner, I come before my God.

21. SINNER IS WHAT I AM
    1 John 1:5-2:17
    Focus: I am sinner and saved.

22. FORGIVENESS
    Matthew 18:21-35
    Focus: God's forgiveness calls for my own forgiving.

23. JUDGMENT
    Matthew 25:31-46
    Focus: God's compassion sets the pattern for my own compassion.

24. JUDGMENT
    Matthew 7:1-23
    Focus: God's judgment looks to the whole of my life.

25. PRAYER OF A SINNER
    Psalm 38
    Focus: I cry out to God in my need.

26. PRAYER OF REPENTANCE
    Psalm 51
    Focus: I ask for mercy.

27. DEATH TO SIN
    Romans 6
    Focus: Sin is possible, but I choose Christ.

28. THE RAISING OF LAZARUS
    John 11:1-44
    Focus: One who is dead is raised up by Christ.

[261]

THE MYSTERIES OF THE LIFE OF CHRIST OUR LORD

Note. It is to be noted in all the following Mysteries, that all the words which are inclosed in parentheses [1] are from the Gospel itself and not those which are outside.

And in each Mystery, for the most part, three Points will be found to meditate and contemplate on with greater ease.

[262]

OF THE ANNUNCIATION OF OUR LADY

St. Luke writes in the first Chapter [26–39].

First Point. The first Point is that the Angel St. Gabriel, saluting Our Lady, announced to her the Conception of Christ our Lord. "The Angel entering where Mary was, saluted her saying: 'Hail full of grace. Thou shalt conceive in thy womb and shalt bring forth a son.'"

Second Point. The second, the Angel confirms what he said to Our Lady, telling of the conception of St. John Baptist, saying to her: "'And behold thy cousin Elizabeth hath conceived a son in her old age.'"

Third Point. The third, Our Lady answered the Angel: "'Behold the handmaid of the Lord: be it done to me according to thy word!'"

---

[1] *For the parentheses of the Mss. quotation marks have been substituted.*

C. The Mysteries of the Life of Our Lord—Second Week

THE MYSTERIES OF THE LIFE OF CHRIST OUR LORD   [261]

SCRIPTURE TEXTS

29. THE ANNUNCIATION TO OUR LADY   [262]
Luke 1:26-38
Focus: God's word calls forth Mary's response.

[263]

OF THE VISITATION OF OUR LADY TO ELIZABETH

St. Luke speaks in the first Chapter [39–57].

First Point. First: As Our Lady visited Elizabeth, St. John Baptist, being in his mother's womb, felt the visitation which Our Lady made. "And when Elizabeth heard the salutation of Our Lady, the infant leaped in her womb. And Elizabeth, full of the Holy Ghost, cried out with a loud voice, and said: ' Blessed be thou among women and blessed be the fruit of thy womb ! ' "

Second Point. Second: Our Lady sings the canticle, saying: " ' My soul doth magnify the Lord ! ' "

Third Point. Third: "Mary abode with Elizabeth about three months: and then she returned to her house."

[264]

OF THE BIRTH OF CHRIST OUR LORD

St. Luke speaks in the second Chapter [1–15].

First Point. First: Our Lady and her husband Joseph go from Nazareth to Bethlehem. "Joseph went up from Galilee to Bethlehem, to acknowledge subjection to Caesar, with Mary his spouse and wife, already with child."

Second Point. Second: "She brought forth her first-born Son and wrapped Him up with swaddling clothes and laid Him in the manger."

Third Point. Third: "There came a multitude of the heavenly army, which said: ' Glory be to God in the heavens. ' "

30. THE VISITATION OF OUR LADY TO ELIZABETH   [263]
Luke 1:39-56
Focus: Mary rejoices in being the Christ-
bearer.

31. BIRTH OF CHRIST OUR LORD   [264]
Luke 2:1-14
Focus: I can simply gaze upon God-become-
man.

[265]
OF THE SHEPHERDS

St. Luke writes in the second Chapter [8–21].

First Point. First: The birth of Christ our Lord is manifested to the Shepherds by the Angel. " 'I manifest to you great joy, for this day is born the Saviour of the world.' "

Second Point. Second: The Shepherds go to Bethlehem. "They came with haste and they found Mary and Joseph, and the infant put in the manger."

Third Point. Third: "The Shepherds returned glorifying and praising the Lord."

[266]
OF THE CIRCUMCISION

St. Luke writes in the second Chapter [21].

First Point. First: They circumcised the Child Jesus.

Second Point. Second: "His Name was called Jesus, which was called by the Angel, before He was conceived in the womb."

Third Point. Third: They gave back the Child to His Mother, who had compassion for the Blood which came from her Son.

[267]
OF THE THREE MAGI KINGS

St. Matthew writes in the second Chapter [1–13].

First Point. First: The three Magi Kings, guiding themselves by the star, came to adore Jesus, saying: " 'We have seen His star in the East and are come to adore Him.' "

Second Point. Second: They adored Him and offered gifts to Him. "Falling down on the earth, they adored Him, and

32. THE SHEPHERDS   [265]
Luke 2:8-20
Focus: how the good news affects men.

33. THE CIRCUMCISION   [266]
Luke 2:21
Focus: the name Jesus has so much meaning.

34. THE MAGI   [267]
Matthew 2:1-12
Focus: the great faith called forth in the
Magi.

they offered Him gifts, gold, frankincense and myrrh."

Third Point. Third: "They received answer while sleeping that they should not return to Herod, and went back by another way to their country."

[268]   OF THE PURIFICATION OF OUR LADY AND PRESENTATION OF THE CHILD JESUS

St. Luke writes, Chapter 2 [23–39].

First Point. First: They bring the Child Jesus to the Temple, that He may be presented to the Lord as first-born; and they offer for Him "a pair of turtle doves or two young pigeons."

Second Point. Second: Simeon coming to the Temple "took Him into his arms" saying: "'Now Thou dost dismiss Thy servant, O Lord, in peace!'"

Third Point. Third: Anna "coming afterwards confessed to the Lord, and spoke of Him to all that were hoping for the redemption of Israel."

[269]   OF THE FLIGHT TO EGYPT

St. Matthew writes in the second Chapter [13–16].

First Point. First: Herod wanted to kill the Child Jesus, and so killed the Innocents, and before their death the Angel warned Joseph to fly into Egypt: "'Arise and take the Child and His Mother, and fly to Egypt.'"

Second Point. Second: He departed for Egypt. "Who arising by night departed to Egypt."

Third Point. Third: He was there until the death of Herod.

35. THE PURIFICATION OF OUR LADY AND THE   [268]
PRESENTATION OF THE CHILD JESUS
Luke 2:22-39
Focus: the examples of Mary, Jesus, Simeon
and Anna are each a call to faith.

36. THE FLIGHT INTO EGYPT   [269]
Matthew 2:13-18
Focus:the care of God's providence is made
evident.

[270]

OF HOW CHRIST OUR LORD RETURNED FROM EGYPT

St. Matthew writes in the second Chapter [19–23].

First Point. First: The Angel warns Joseph to return to Israel. "'Arise and take the Child and His Mother and go to the land of Israel.'"

Second Point. Second: Rising, he came to the land of Israel.

Third Point. Third: Because Archelaus, son of Herod, was reigning in Judea, he withdrew into Nazareth.

[271]

OF THE LIFE OF CHRIST OUR LORD FROM TWELVE TO THIRTY YEARS

St. Luke writes in the second Chapter [51, 52].

First Point. First: He was obedient to His parents: "He advanced in wisdom, age and grace."

Second Point. Second: It appears that He exercised the trade of carpenter, as St. Mark shows he means in the sixth chapter. "'Perhaps this is that carpenter?'"

[272]

OF THE COMING OF CHRIST TO THE TEMPLE WHEN HE WAS OF THE AGE OF TWELVE YEARS

St. Luke writes in the second Chapter [42–51].

First Point. First: Christ our Lord, of the age of twelve years, went up from Nazareth to Jerusalem.

Second Point. Second: Christ our Lord remained in Jerusalem, and His parents did not know it.

Third Point. Third: The three days passed, they found Him disputing in the

37. THE RETURN FROM EGYPT   [270]
               Matthew 2:19-23
          Focus: God's work is seen in ordinary human
             decisions.

38. THE LIFE OF CHRIST OUR LORD FROM THE   [271]
    AGE OF TWELVE TO THE AGE OF THIRTY
               Luke 2:51-52
          Focus: How ordinary is the growth of Jesus.

39. JESUS GOES UP TO THE TEMPLE AT THE   [272]
    AGE OF TWELVE
               Luke 2:41-50
          Focus: Jesus has a sense of a special call.

Temple, and seated in the midst of the doctors, and His parents asking Him where He had been, He answered: "'Did you not know that it behooves Me to be in the things which are My Father's?'"

[273] ### OF HOW CHRIST WAS BAPTIZED

St. Matthew writes in the third Chapter [13–17].

First Point. First: Christ our Lord, after having taken leave of His Blessed Mother, came from Nazareth to the River Jordan, where St. John Baptist was.

Second Point. Second: St. John baptized Christ our Lord, and wanting to excuse himself, thinking himself unworthy of baptizing Him, Christ said to him: "'Do this for the present, for so it is necessary that we fulfill all justice.'"

Third Point. Third: "The Holy Spirit came and the voice of the Father from heaven affirming: 'This is My beloved Son, in Whom I am well pleased.'"

[274] ### OF HOW CHRIST WAS TEMPTED

St. Luke writes in the fourth Chapter [1–14] and St. Matthew fourth Chapter [1–12].

First Point. First: After being baptized, He went to the Desert, where He fasted forty days and forty nights.

Second Point. Second: He was tempted by the enemy three times. "The tempter coming to Him said to Him: 'If Thou be the Son of God, say that these stones be turned into bread.' 'Cast Thyself down from here.' 'If prostrate on the earth Thou wilt adore me, I will give Thee all this which Thou seest.'"

40. THE BAPTISM OF CHRIST   [273]
                Matthew 3:13-17
        Focus: Jesus is clearly called forth by his
        Father.

41. THE TEMPTATION OF CHRIST   [274]
            Luke 4:1-13; Matthew 4:1-11
        Focus: the reality of temptation is present
        in Christ's calling.

Third Point. Third: "The Angels came and ministered to Him."

[275]   OF THE CALL OF THE APOSTLES

First Point. First: it seems that [1] St. Peter and St. Andrew were called three times: first, to some knowledge; this is clear from St. John in the first Chapter: secondly, to follow Christ in some way with the purpose of returning to possess what they had left, as St. Luke says in the fifth Chapter: thirdly, to follow Christ our Lord forever, as St. Matthew says in the fourth Chapter and St. Mark in the first.

Second Point. Second: He called Philip, as is in the first Chapter of St. John, and Matthew as Matthew himself says in the ninth Chapter.

Third Point. Third: He called the other Apostles, of whose special call the Gospel does not make mention.

And three other things also would be to be considered:

The first, how the Apostles were of uneducated and low condition;

The second, the dignity to which they were so sweetly called;

The third, the gifts and graces by which they were raised above all the Fathers of the New and Old Testaments.

[276]   OF THE FIRST MIRACLE
PERFORMED AT THE MARRIAGE OF CANA, GALILEE

St. John writes Chapter 2 [1–12].

First Point. First: Christ our Lord was invited with His Disciples to the marriage.

Second Point. Second: The Mother tells her Son of the failure of the wine,

---

[1] It seems that *is added in the hand of St. Ignatius.*

42. THE VOCATION OF THE APOSTLES   [275]
John 1:35-51; Luke 5:1-11; Matthew 4:18-22;
Matthew 9:9; Mark 1:16-20
Focus: Jesus calls in a special way to certain
persons.

43. THE FIRST MIRACLE PERFORMED AT THE   [276]
MARRIAGE FEAST OF CANA IN GALILEE
John 2:1-11
Focus: Mary's faith calls forth Jesus' re-
sponse.

saying: "'They have no wine,'" and bade the servants: "'Whatsoever He shall say to you, do ye.'"

Third Point. Third: "He changed the water into wine and manifested His glory, and His Disciples believed in Him."

[277]   OF HOW CHRIST CAST OUT OF THE TEMPLE
THOSE WHO WERE SELLING

St. John writes Chapter 2 [13–18].

First Point. First: With a whip made of cords, He cast out of the Temple all those who were selling.

Second Point. Second: He turned over the tables and money of the rich bankers who were in the Temple.

Third Point. Third: To the poor who sold doves, He mildly said: "'Take these things from here, and make not My house a house of traffic.'"

[278]   OF THE SERMON WHICH CHRIST MADE ON
THE MOUNT

St. Matthew writes in the fifth Chapter [1–48].

First Point. First: To His beloved Disciples He speaks apart about the Eight Beatitudes: "'Blessed the poor of spirit, the meek, the merciful, those who weep, those who suffer hunger and thirst for justice, the clean of heart, the peaceful, and those who suffer persecution.'"

Second Point. Second: He exhorts them to use their talents well: "'So let your light shine before men, that they may see your good works and glorify your Father Who is in the heavens.'"

Third Point. Third: He shows Himself not a transgressor, but a perfector of the law; explaining the precept of not killing, not committing fornication, not being guilty of perjury, and of loving enemies.

44. CHRIST CASTS THE SELLERS FROM THE   [277]
    TEMPLE
               John 2:13-22
      Focus: Jesus shows forth zeal to carry out
      his Father's will.

45. THE SERMON ON THE MOUNT   [278]
             Matthew 5
    Focus: The strategy of Christ is presented.

" ' I say to you that you love your enemies and do good to them that hate you.' "

[279]

OF HOW CHRIST OUR LORD MADE THE TEMPEST OF THE SEA BE CALM

St. Matthew writes Chapter 8 [23–28].

First Point. First: Christ our Lord being asleep at sea, a great tempest arose.

Second Point. Second: His Disciples, frightened, awakened Him. Whom He reprehends for the little faith which they had, saying to them: " ' What do you fear, ye of little faith! ' "

Third Point. Third: He commanded the winds and the sea to cease: and, so ceasing, the sea became calm: at which the men wondered, saying: " ' Who is this whom the wind and the sea obey? ' "

[280]

OF HOW CHRIST WALKED ON THE SEA

St. Matthew writes Chapter 14 [22–34].

First Point. First: Christ our Lord being on the mountain, made His Disciples go to the little boat. And having dismissed the multitude, He commenced to pray alone.

Second Point. Second: The little boat was beaten by the waves. To which Christ came walking on the water; and the Disciples thought it was an apparition.

Third Point. Third: Christ saying to them: " ' It is I, fear not,' " St. Peter, by His command, came to Him walking on the water. Doubting, he commenced to sink, but Christ our Lord freed him and reprehended him for his little faith, and then, as He entered into the little boat, the wind ceased.

46. CHRIST CALMS THE STORM   [279]
                    Matthew 8:23-27
        Focus: Christ shows forth the power of God.

47. CHRIST WALKS ON THE WATER   [280]
                    Matthew 14:22-33
        Focus: Christ calls to an ever greater faith.

[281]

OF HOW THE APOSTLES WERE SENT
TO PREACH

St. Matthew writes in the tenth Chapter [1–17].

First Point. . First: Christ called His beloved Disciples and gave them power to cast out the demons from human bodies and to cure all the diseases.

Second Point. Second: He teaches them of prudence and patience: "'Behold, I send you as sheep in the midst of wolves. Be ye therefore wise as serpents and simple as doves.'"

Third Point. Third: He gives them the way to go. "'Do not want to possess gold nor silver: what you have freely received, freely give.'" And He gave them matter to preach. "'Going you shall preach, saying: 'The Kingdom of Heaven has approached.'"

[282]

OF THE CONVERSION OF MAGDALEN

St. Luke writes in the seventh Chapter [36–50].

First Point. First: Magdalen enters where Christ our Lord is seated at the table in the house of the Pharisee. She bore a vase of alabaster full of ointment.

Second Point. Second: Standing behind the Lord near His feet, she commenced to wash them with tears and dried them with the hairs of her head, and kissed His feet and anointed them with ointment.

Third Point. Third: When the Pharisee accused Magdalen, Christ speaks in her defence, saying: "'Many sins are forgiven her because she loves much.' And He said to the woman: 'Thy faith hath made thee safe: go in peace.'"

48. THE APOSTLES ARE SENT TO PREACH   [281]
Matthew 10:1-16
Focus: Jesus shares his mission.

49. THE CONVERSION OF MAGDALENE   [282]
Luke 7:36-50
Focus: Jesus calls to conversion by love.

[283]

OF HOW CHRIST OUR LORD GAVE TO EAT TO FIVE THOUSAND MEN

St. Matthew writes in the fourteenth Chapter [13–22].

First Point. First: The Disciples, as it was getting late, ask Christ to dismiss the multitude of men who were with Him.

Second Point. Second: Christ our Lord commands that they bring Him bread, and commanded that they should be seated at the table, and blessed and broke and gave the bread to His Disciples, and the Disciples to the multitude.

Third Point. Third: "They did eat and were filled and there were twelve baskets over."

[284]

OF THE TRANSFIGURATION OF CHRIST

St. Matthew writes in the seventeenth Chapter [1–14].

First Point. First: Taking along His beloved Disciples, Peter, James, John, Christ our Lord was transfigured, and His face did shine as the sun, and His garments as the snow.

Second Point. Second: He was speaking with Moses and Elias.

Third Point. Third: St. Peter saying that they would make three tabernacles, a voice from heaven sounded, which said: "'This is My beloved Son, hear ye Him!'" When His Disciples heard this voice, they fell for fear on their faces; and Christ our Lord touched them and said to them: "'Arise and fear not. Tell this vision to no one until the Son of Man be risen.'"

50. CHRIST FEEDS THE FIVE THOUSAND   [283]
Matthew 14:13-21
Focus: Jesus' concern is shown for all the
people.

51. THE TRANSFIGURATION   [284]
Matthew 17:1-9
Focus: Jesus has his own religious experi-
ence.

[285]   OF THE RESURRECTION OF LAZARUS

John, Chapter 11 [1–46].

First Point. First: Martha and Mary sent word to Christ our Lord of the illness of Lazarus. Knowing it, He delayed for two days, that the miracle might be more evident.

Second Point. Second: Before He raises him, He asks the one and the other to believe, saying: "'I am the resurrection and life; he who believeth in Me, although he be dead, shall live.'"

Third Point. Third: He raises him, after having wept and prayed. And the manner of raising him was by commanding: "'Lazarus, come forth!'"

[286]   OF THE SUPPER AT BETHANY

Matthew, Chapter 26 [1–14].

First Point. First: The Lord sups in the house of Simon the Leper, along with Lazarus.

Second Point. Second: Mary pours the ointment on the head of Christ.

Third Point. Third: Judas murmurs, saying: "'For what is this waste of ointment?'" But He a second time excuses Magdalen, saying: "'Why are you troublesome to this woman? for she hath wrought a good work upon Me.'"

[287]   PALM SUNDAY

Matthew, Chapter 21 [1–12].

First Point. First: The Lord sends for the ass and the foal, saying: "Loose them and bring them to Me, and if any one shall say anything to you, say ye that the Lord hath need of them, and forthwith he will let them go."

Second Point. Second: He mounted upon the ass, which was covered with the garments of the Apostles.

52. THE RAISING OF LAZARUS   [285]
                John 11:1-45
      Focus: Jesus is seen as the Resurrection and
          the Life.

53. THE SUPPER AT BETHANY   [286]
              Matthew 26:6-10
      Focus: Jesus accepts a love gesture.

54. PALM SUNDAY   [287]
              Matthew 21:1-17
      Focus: Jesus enters Jerusalem as King and
          Messiah.

Third Point. Third: They went out to receive Him, strewing in the way their garments and the branches of the trees, saying: "'Save us, Son of David, blessed is He that cometh in the name of the Lord: Save us in the heights!'"

[288]

OF THE PREACHING IN THE TEMPLE

Luke, Chapter 19 [47, 48].

First Point. First: He was every day teaching in the Temple.

Second Point. Second: The preaching finished, since there was no one who would receive Him in Jerusalem, He used to return to Bethany.

[289]

OF THE SUPPER

Matthew 26; John 13.

First Point. First: He ate the Paschal Lamb with His twelve Apostles, to whom He foretold His death. "'In truth, I say to you that one of you is to sell Me.'"

Second Point. Second: He washed the Disciples' feet, even those of Judas, commencing from St. Peter, who, considering the Majesty of the Lord and his own baseness, not wanting to consent, said: "Lord, dost Thou wash my feet?" But St. Peter did not know that in that He gave an example of humility, and for this He said: "'I have given you an example, that you may do as I did.'"

Third Point. Third: He instituted the most sacred sacrifice of the Eucharist, to be the greatest mark of His love, saying: "'Take and eat.'" The Supper finished, Judas went forth to sell Christ our Lord.

55. JESUS PREACHES IN THE TEMPLE   [288]
               Luke 19:47-48
        Focus: Jesus remains faithful to his mission.

D. The Mysteries of the Life of Our Lord—Third Week:

56. THE LAST SUPPER   [289]
          Matthew 26:20-30; John 13:1-30
        Focus: Jesus serves in giving himself totally.

[290]

OF THE MYSTERIES DONE FROM THE SUPPER TO THE GARDEN, INCLUSIVE

Matthew, Chapter 26, and Mark, Chapter 14.

First Point. First: The Supper finished, and singing the hymn, the Lord went to Mount Olivet with His Disciples, who were full of fear; and leaving the eight in Gethsemani, He said: "'Sit ye here till I go yonder to pray.'"

Second Point. Second: Accompanied by St. Peter, St. James and St. John, He prayed three times to the Lord, saying: "'Father, if it be possible, let this chalice pass from Me. Nevertheless, let not My will be done, but Thine.'" And being in agony, He prayed the longer."

Third Point. Third: He came into such fear, that He said: "'My soul is sorrowful unto death,'" and He sweated blood so plentiful, that St. Luke says: "His sweat was as drops of blood which were running on the earth;" which supposes that the garments were already full of blood.

[291]

OF THE MYSTERIES DONE FROM THE GARDEN TO THE HOUSE OF ANNAS, INCLUSIVE

Matthew 26, Luke 22, Mark 15.

First Point. First: The Lord lets Himself be kissed by Judas and taken as a robber, to whom He said: "'You have come out as to a robber to apprehend Me with clubs and arms; when I was daily with you in the Temple teaching and you did not take Me.'" And He saying: "'Whom seek ye?'" the enemies fell on the earth.

Second Point. Second: St. Peter wounded a servant of the High Priest, and the meek

57. FROM THE SUPPER TO THE AGONY INCLUSIVE   [290]
Matthew 26:30-46; Mark 14:32-44
Focus: Jesus seeks only the will of his Father.

58. FROM THE GARDEN TO THE HOUSE   [291]
OF ANNAS INCLUSIVE
Matthew 26:47-58; Luke 22:47-57
Mark 14:44-54 and 66-68
Focus: Jesus lives his passion.

Lord said to Peter: "'Return thy sword into its place,'" and He healed the wound of the servant.

Third Point. Third: Left by His Disciples, He is taken to Annas, where St. Peter, who had followed Him from afar, denied Him once, and a blow was given Christ by one saying to Him: "'Answerest Thou the High Priest so?'"

[292]

OF THE MYSTERIES DONE FROM THE HOUSE OF ANNAS TO THE HOUSE OF CAIPHAS, INCLUSIVE

First Point. First: They take Him bound from the house of Annas to the house of Caiphas, where St. Peter denied Him twice, and looked at by the Lord, going forth he wept bitterly.

Second Point. Second: Jesus was all that night bound.

Third Point. Third: Besides, those who held Him captive mocked Him and struck Him and covered His face and gave Him buffets and asked Him: "'Prophesy to us, who is he that struck Thee?'" and like things, blaspheming against Him.

[293]

OF THE MYSTERIES DONE FROM THE HOUSE OF CAIPHAS TO THAT OF PILATE, INCLUSIVE

Matthew 26, Luke 23, Mark 15.
First Point. First: The whole multitude of the Jews take Him to Pilate and accuse Him before him, saying: "'We have found that this man tried to ruin our people and forbade to pay tribute to Caesar.'"

Second Point. Second: Pilate, after having examined Him once and again, said: "'I find no fault.'"

Third Point. Third: The robber Ba-

59. FROM THE HOUSE OF ANNAS TO THE   [292]
HOUSE OF CAIAPHAS INCLUSIVE
Matthew 26; Mark 14;
Luke 22; John 18
Focus: Jesus lives his passion.

60. FROM THE HOUSE OF CAIAPHAS TO THE   [293]
HOUSE OF PILATE INCLUSIVE
Matthew 27; Luke 23; Mark 15
Focus: Jesus lives his passion.

rabbas was preferred to Him. "They all cried, saying: 'Give us not this man, but Barabbas!'"

[294]   OF THE MYSTERIES DONE FROM THE HOUSE
          OF PILATE TO THAT OF HEROD

First Point. First: Pilate sent Jesus, a Galilean, to Herod, Tetrarch of Galilee.

Second Point. Second: Herod, curious, questioned Him much and He answered him nothing, although the Scribes and Priests were accusing Him constantly.

Third Point. Third: Herod despised Him with his army, clothing Him with a white garment.

[295]   OF THE MYSTERIES DONE FROM THE HOUSE
          OF HEROD TO THAT OF PILATE

Matthew 27, Luke 23, Mark 15, and John 19.

First Point. First: Herod sends Him back to Pilate. By this they were made friends, who before were enemies.

Second Point. Second: Pilate took Jesus and scourged Him; and the soldiers made a crown of thorns and put it on His head, and they clothed Him with purple and came to Him and said: "'Hail, King of the Jews!'", and they gave Him buffets.

Third Point. Third: He brought Him forth in the presence of all. "Then Jesus went forth crowned with thorns and clothed with a purple garment, and Pilate said to them: 'Here is the Man!'" and when the Priests saw Him, they shouted, saying: "'Crucify, crucify Him!'"

61. FROM THE HOUSE OF PILATE TO THE   [294]
    HOUSE OF HEROD
                  Luke 23:6-11
          Focus: Jesus lives his passion.

62. FROM THE HOUSE OF HEROD TO THAT OF   [295]
    PILATE
                  Matthew 27: Luke 23;
                  Mark 15; John 19
          Focus: Jesus lives his passion.

[296]

OF THE MYSTERIES DONE FROM THE HOUSE OF PILATE TO THE CROSS, INCLUSIVE

John 19 [15–20].

First Point. First: Pilate, seated as judge, delivered Jesus to them to crucify Him, after the Jews had denied Him for king, saying: "'We have no king but Caesar!'"

Second Point. Second: He took the Cross on His shoulders and not being able to carry it, Simon of Cyrene was constrained to carry it after Jesus.

Third Point. Third: They crucified Him between two thieves, setting this title: "Jesus of Nazareth, King of the Jews."

[297]

OF THE MYSTERIES ON THE CROSS

John 19 [25–37].

First Point. First: He spoke seven words on the Cross: He prayed for those who were crucifying Him; He pardoned the thief; He recommended St. John to His Mother and His Mother to St. John; He said with a loud voice: "'I thirst,'" and they gave Him gall and vinegar; He said that He was abandoned; He said: "It is consummated"; He said: "Father, into Thy hands I commend My spirit!"

Second Point. Second: The sun was darkened, the stones broken, the graves opened, the veil of the Temple was rent in two from above below.

Third Point. Third: They blaspheme Him, saying: "'Thou wert He who destroyest the Temple of God; come down from the Cross.'" His garments were divided; His side, struck with the lance, sent forth water and blood.

63. FROM THE HOUSE OF PILATE TO THE   [296]
    CROSS INCLUSIVE
John 19:13-22
Focus: Jesus lives his passion.

64. JESUS DIES UPON THE CROSS   [297]
John 19:23-27; Matthew 27:35-52;
Mark 15:24-38; Luke 23:34-46
Focus: Jesus fulfills the Father's will to the
very end.

[298]

OF THE MYSTERIES FROM THE CROSS TO THE SEPULCHRE, INCLUSIVE

Ibidem.

First Point. First: He was let down from the Cross by Joseph and Nicodemus, in presence of His sorrowful Mother.

Second Point. Second: The Body was carried to the Sepulchre and anointed and buried.

Third Point. Third: Guards were set.

[299]

OF THE RESURRECTION OF CHRIST OUR LORD
OF HIS FIRST APPARITION

First Point. First: He appeared to the Virgin Mary. This, although it is not said in Scripture, is included in saying that He appeared to so many others, because Scripture supposes that we have understanding,[1] as it is written: " 'Are you also without understanding?' "

[300]

OF THE SECOND APPARITION

Mark, Chapter 16 [9].

First Point. First: Mary Magdalen, Mary, the mother of James, and Salome come very[2] early to the Sepulchre saying: " 'Who shall lift for us the stone from the door of the Sepulchre?' "

Second Point. Second: They see the stone lifted, and the Angel, who says: " 'You seek Jesus of Nazareth. He is already risen, He is not here.' "

Third Point. Third: He appeared to Mary, who remained about the Sepulchre after the others had gone.

---

[1] Understanding *is added, apparently in St. Ignatius'* hand.

[2] Very *is added, perhaps in St. Ignatius' hand.*

65. FROM THE CROSS TO THE SEPULCHER [298]
    INCLUSIVE
            Ibidem
        Focus: We enter into the sense of loss,
        emptiness, waiting.

E. The Mysteries of the Life of Our Lord—Fourth Week:

66. THE RESURRECTION OF CHRIST OUR [299]
    LORD—THE FIRST APPARITION
            No Scripture text
        Focus: Jesus is seen in his consoling role for
        Mary his mother.

67. THE SECOND APPARITION [300]
            Mark 16:1-11
        Focus: "He is risen."

[301]

OF THE THIRD APPARITION

St. Matthew, last Chapter.

First Point. First: These Maries go from the Sepulchre with fear and joy, wanting to announce to the Disciples the Resurrection of the Lord.

Second Point. Second: Christ our Lord appeared to them on the way, saying to them: "Hail:" and they approached and threw themselves at His feet and adored Him.

Third Point. Third: Jesus says to them: "'Fear not! Go and tell My brethren that they go into Galilee, for there they shall see Me.'"

[302]

OF THE FOURTH APPARITION

Last Chapter of Luke [12, 34].

First Point. First: Having heard from the women that Christ was risen, St. Peter went quickly to the Sepulchre.

Second Point. Second: Entering into the Sepulchre, he saw only the cloths with which the Body of Christ our Lord had been covered, and nothing else.

Third Point. Third: As St. Peter was thinking of these things, Christ appeared to Him, and therefore the Apostles said: "'Truly the Lord has risen and appeared to Simon.'"

[303]

OF THE FIFTH APPARITION

In the last Chapter of St. Luke.

First Point. First: He appeared to the Disciples who were going to Emmaus, talking of Christ.

Second Point. Second: He reproves them, showing by the Scriptures that Christ had to die and rise again: "'O foolish and slow of heart to believe all that the Prophets have spoken! Was it not

68. THE THIRD APPARITION [301]
Matthew 28
Focus: Jesus is the consoler.

69. THE FOURTH APPARITION [302]
Luke 24:9-12 and 33-34
Focus: how wonderful is the resurrection of the Lord.

70. THE FIFTH APPARITION [303]
Luke 24
Focus: Christ is the consoler.

necessary that Christ should suffer and so enter into His glory?'"

Third Point. Third: At their prayer, He lingers there, and was with them until, in giving them Communion, He disappeared. And they, returning, told the Disciples how they had known Him in the Communion.

[304]

OF THE SIXTH APPARITION

John, Chapter 20 [19–24].

First Point. First: The Disciples, except St. Thomas, were gathered together for fear of the Jews.

Second Point. Second: Jesus appeared to them, the doors being shut, and being in the midst of them, He says: "'Peace be with you!'"

Third Point. Third: He gives them the Holy Ghost, saying to them: "'Receive ye the Holy Ghost: to those whose sins you shall forgive, to them they shall be forgiven.'"

[305]

THE SEVENTH APPARITION

John 20 [24–30].

First Point. First: St. Thomas, incredulous because he was absent from the preceding apparition, says: "If I do not see Him, I will not believe."

Second Point. Second: Jesus appears to them eight days from that, the doors being shut, and says to St. Thomas: "'Put here thy finger and see the truth; and be not incredulous, but believing.'"

Third Point. Third: St. Thomas believed, saying: "'My Lord and my God!'" Christ said to him: "'Blessed are those who have not seen and have believed.'"

71. THE SIXTH APPARITION [304]
John 20:19-23
Focus: Christ is the life-giver.

72. THE SEVENTH APPARITION [305]
John 20:24-29
Focus: faith in the Lord Jesus is seeing and
not seeing.

[306]   **OF THE EIGHTH APPARITION**

John, last Chapter [1–24].

First Point. First: Jesus appears to seven of His Disciples who were fishing, and had taken nothing all night; and spreading the net by His command, "They were not able to draw it out for the multitude of the fishes."

Second Point. Second: By this miracle St. John knew Him and said to St. Peter: "'It is the Lord!'" He cast himself into the sea and came to Christ.

Third Point. Third: He gave them to eat part of a fish roasted, and a comb of honey, and recommended the sheep to St. Peter, having first examined him three times on charity, and says to him: "'Feed My sheep!'"

[307]   **OF THE NINTH APPARITION**

Matthew, last Chapter [16–end].

First Point. First: The Disciples, by command of the Lord, go to Mt. Thabor.

Second Point. Second: Christ appears to them and says: "'All power is given to Me in heaven and on earth.'"

Third Point. Third: He sent them through all the world to preach, saying: "'Go and teach ye all nations, baptizing them in the name of the Father and of the Son and of the Holy Ghost.'"

[308]   **OF THE TENTH APPARITION**

In the First Epistle to the Corinthians, Chapter 15 [7]. "Afterwards He was seen by more than five hundred brethren together."

73. THE EIGHTH APPARITION   [306]
                John 21:1-17
        Focus: Christ is the consoler.

74. THE NINTH APPARITION   [307]
              Matthew 28:16-20
        Focus: Christ sends out his followers.

75. THE TENTH APPARITION   [308]
                 1 Cor 15:6
        Focus: Christ is the consoler.

[309]

OF THE ELEVENTH APPARITION

In the First Epistle to the Corinthians, Chapter 15 [7]. "Afterwards He appeared to St. James."

[310]

OF THE TWELFTH APPARITION

He appeared to Joseph of Arimathea, as is piously meditated and is read in the lives of the Saints.[1]

[311]

OF THE THIRTEENTH APPARITION

First Epistle to the Corinthians, Chapter 15 [8]. He appeared to St. Paul after the Ascension. " 'Last of all, He appeared to me, as one born out of due time.' "

He appeared also in soul to the Holy Fathers of Limbo, and after taking them out and having taken His Body again, He appeared to the Disciples many times, and dealt with them.

[312]

OF THE ASCENSION OF CHRIST OUR LORD

Acts 1 [1–12].

First Point. First: After He appeared for the space of forty days to the Apostles, giving many arguments and doing many signs, and speaking of the kingdom of God, He bade them await in Jerusalem the Holy Ghost promised.

Second Point. Second: He brought them out to Mt. Olivet, and in their presence He was raised up and a cloud made Him disappear from their eyes.

Third Point. Third: They looking to heaven, the Angels say to them: " ' Men of Galilee, why stand you looking to heaven? This Jesus, Who is taken from your eyes to heaven, shall so come as you saw Him go into heaven.' "

[1] Is piously meditated and is read in the lives of the Saints *is in the hand of St. Ignatius, replacing words which were apparently* says the Gospel of Judea.

[313-
336]

GUIDELINES FOR THE DISCERNMENT OF SPIRITS

Preliminary Note: On the use of "spirits," good and evil.

"Discernment of spirits" is a venerable phrase of Christian spiritual tradition. From the action of good or evil spirits upon one result "movements of one's heart or spirit," "motions affecting one's interior life," "a certain impetus in one's life," "a feeling for or against some course of action," and so on. The descriptive words "good" and "evil" as applied to "spirits" are used to designate primarily the source or cause of the movement or feeling as a good or an evil spirit. What we experience, however, is that good spirits lead a person in a good direction towards a good goal. Evil spirits make use of evil directions, and even sometimes of what are at first good directions, to accomplish an evil end.

Although the importance of these movements comes in the direction which they give to our lives, we are necessarily concerned about recognizing their good or evil source, especially in view of the possible deception of an apparently good direction. In the light of modern psychology, we have some indications of the great complexity of human motivations. Added to this complexity of human motivation, we Christians live in a faith-world which acknowledges the unfathomable power of evil personified in Satan and the damned of hell and the even more mysterious power of good focused in God and in the communion of saints. And so when we attempt to say something not only about the direction of these spirits but also about what the sources of these good and evil spirits or motions are, we can still find helpful a scheme adapted and expanded from the traditional Ignatian division in [32]:
Good spirits and evil spirits come from
(1) within our very selves, or
(2) outside of us, from
(a) our fellow men, or
(b) power more than human.

Although as redeemed sinners we can confess that both good and evil motions emanate from within us, we still stand amazed at both the good and the evil which comes forth from the heart of us human beings. Like St. Paul in his seventh chapter of the Letter to the Romans, we suffer from the divisions we feel within our very selves. In fact, we commonly feel more comfortable to be able to blame evil on someone or something outside of ourselves. Even the first sin of man and woman is pictured in such a way in the third chapter of Genesis when Adam attempts to shift the blame to Eve, and Eve looks to the serpent. Yet without in any way lessening our own potential human malice, we have experientially as well as scripturally the evidence of a power of evil that is bigger than any one person or group of persons. Just as our fellowmen can influence our choices and action towards wrong, so too the "more than human" power of evil is destructive and deadly in its enticements and enslavements. While our fellowmen can also be an influence for good, we know similarly from experience and from Scripture another power of good, which comes from God himself directly intervening in our lives as well as the continuing intercession of the saints who have gone before us.

In the following guidelines for discerning spirits, an attempt is made to give helps to develop an ability to recognize ever earlier the direction of certain movements or feelings in our lives, and so to be able to follow or reject them almost in their very sources.

PART I. Guidelines Suitable Especially for the First Week [313-327]

The statements below are an attempt to present certain norms which might be helpful in understanding different interior movements which happen in the "heart" of man and woman. By the grace of God, we are meant to recognize those that are good so that we might let them give direction to our lives and those

RULES

[313]

FOR PERCEIVING AND KNOWING IN SOME MANNER

THE DIFFERENT MOVEMENTS WHICH ARE CAUSED IN THE SOUL

THE GOOD, TO RECEIVE THEM, AND THE BAD TO REJECT THEM. AND THEY ARE MORE PROPER FOR THE FIRST WEEK.

[314] **First Rule.** The first Rule: In the persons who go from mortal sin to mortal sin, the enemy is commonly used to propose to them apparent pleasures, making them imagine sensual delights and pleasures in order to hold them more and make them grow in their vices and sins. In these persons the good spirit uses the opposite method, pricking them and biting their consciences through the process of reason.

[315] **Second Rule.** The second: In the persons who are going on intensely cleansing their sins and rising from good to better in the service of God our Lord, it is the method contrary to that in the first Rule, for then it is the way of the evil spirit to bite, sadden and put obstacles, disquieting with false reasons, that one may not go on; and it is proper to the good to give courage and strength, consolations, tears, inspirations and quiet, easing, and putting away all obstacles, that one may go on in well doing.

that are bad so that we might reject them or turn aside from them.

The norms in this first section are more appropriate to the kind of spiritual experiences associated with the First Week of the Exercises.

A. Two Statements of General Application

1. When we are caught up in a life of sin or perhaps even [314] if we are closed off from God in only one area of our life, the evil spirit is ordinarily accustomed to propose a slothful complacency or a future of ever greater pleasures still to be grasped. He fills our imagination with all kinds of sensual delights so that there is no will or desire to change the evil direction of our life.

The good spirit uses just the opposite method with us. He will try to make us see the absurdity of the direction our life has taken. Little by little an uneasiness described sometimes as the "sting" of conscience comes about and a feeling of remorse sets in.

2. When we are intent upon living a good life and seeking [315] to pursue the lead of God in our life, the tactics of the spirits are just the opposite of those described above.

The evil spirit proposes to us all the problems and difficulties in living a good life. The evil spirit attempts to rouse a false sadness for things which will be missed, to bring about anxiety about perservering when we are so weak, to suggest innumerable roadblocks in walking the way of the Lord. And so the evil spirit tries discouragement and deception to deter us from growing in the Christ-life.

The good spirit, however, strengthens and encourages, consoles and inspires, establishes a peace and sometimes moves to a firm resolve. To lead a good life gives delight and joy, and no obstacle seems to be so formidable that it cannot be faced and overcome. The good spirit thereby continues an upright person's progress in the Lord.

[316]   **Third Rule.** The third: OF SPIRITUAL CON-
SOLATION. I call it consolation when some interior movement in the soul is caused, through
which the soul comes to be inflamed with love
of its Creator and Lord; and when it can in
consequence love no created thing on the face
of the earth in itself, but in the Creator of
them all.

Likewise, when it sheds tears that move to
love of its Lord, whether out of sorrow for one's
sins, or for the Passion of Christ our Lord,
or because of other things directly connected
with His service and praise.

Finally, I call consolation every increase of
hope, faith and charity, and all interior joy
which calls and attracts to heavenly things and
to the salvation of one's soul, quieting it and
giving it peace in its Creator and Lord.

[317]   **Fourth Rule.** The fourth: OF SPIRITUAL
DESOLATION. I call desolation all the contrary
of the third [1] rule, such as darkness [2] of soul,
disturbance in it, movement to things low and
earthly, the unquiet of different agitations and
temptations, moving to want of confidence,
without hope, without love, when one finds
oneself all lazy, tepid, sad, and as if separated
from his Creator and Lord. Because, as
consolation is contrary to desolation, in the
same way the thoughts which come from consolation are contrary to the thoughts which
come from desolation.

[1] Third *is in the Saint's hand, replacing* first.
[2] Darkness *is perhaps in the Saint's handwriting, replacing* blindness.

B. Particular Statements Referring Especially to Persons Intent upon Changing Their Lives and Doing Good.

First of all, two terms should be defined:

3. SPIRITUAL CONSOLATION. This term describes our interior life: [316]

(a) when we find ourselves so on fire with the love of God that neither anything nor anyone presents itself in competition with a total gift of self to God in love. Rather we begin to see everything and everyone in the context of God, their Creator and Lord;

(b) when we are saddened, even to the point of tears, for our infidelity to God but at the same time thankful to know God as Savior. Such consolation often comes in a deep realization of ourselves as sinner before a God who loves us, or in the face of Christ's Passion when we see that Jesus loves his Father and his fellowmen so much, or for any other reason which leads us to praise and thank and serve God all the better;

(c) when we find our life of faith, hope, and love so strengthened and emboldened that the joy of serving God is foremost in our life. More simply said, consolation can be found in any increase of our faith, our hope, and our love. A deep-down peace comes in just "being in my Father's house."

4. SPIRITUAL DESOLATION. This term describes our interior life: [317]

(a) when we find ourselves enmeshed in a certain turmoil of spirit or feel ourselves weighed down by a heavy darkness or weight;

(b) when we experience a lack of faith or hope or love in the very distaste for prayer or for any spiritual activity and we know a certain restlessness in our carrying on in the service of God;

(c) when we experience just the opposite effect of what has been described as spiritual consolation. For we will notice that the thoughts of rebelliousness, despair, or selfishness which arise at the time of desolation are in absolute contrast with the thoughts of the praise and service of God which flow during the time of consolation.

[318]   **Fifth Rule.** The fifth: In time of desolation never to make a change; but to be firm and constant in the resolutions and determination in which one was the day preceding such desolation, or in the determination in which he was in the preceding consolation. Because, as in consolation it is rather the good spirit who guides and counsels us, so in desolation it is the bad, with whose counsels we cannot take a course to decide rightly.

[319]   **Sixth Rule.** The sixth: Although in desolation we ought not to change our first resolutions, it is very helpful intensely to change ourselves against the same desolation, as by insisting more on prayer, meditation, on much examination, and by giving ourselves more scope in some suitable way of doing penance.

[320]   **Seventh Rule.** The seventh: Let him who is in desolation consider how the Lord has left him in trial in his natural powers, in order to resist the different agitations and temptations of the enemy; since he can with the Divine help, which always remains to him, though he does not clearly perceive it: because the Lord has taken from him his great fervor, great love and intense grace, leaving him, however, grace enough for eternal salvation.

Four guidelines dealing with spiritual desolation now follow:

5. When we find ourselves weighed down by a certain deso-   [318]
lation, we should not try to change a previous decision or to
come to a new decision. The reason is that in desolation the evil
spirit is making an attempt to obstruct the good direction of our
life or to change it, and so we would be thwarted from the
gentle lead of God, and what is more conducive to our own
salvation. As a result, at a time of desolation, we hold fast to the
decision which guided us during the time before the desolation
came on us.

6. Although we should not try to make new decisions at a   [319]
time of desolation, we should not just sit back and do nothing.
We are meant to fight off whatever is making us less than we
should be. And so we might try to intensify our prayer, we
might take on some penance, or we might make a closer examination of ourselves and our life of faith.

7. Oftentimes in desolation, we feel that God has left us to   [320]
fend for ourselves. By faith we know that he is always with us
in the strength and power of his grace, but at the time of apparent abandonment we are little aware of his care and concern.
We experience neither the support nor the sweetness of his love,
and our own response lacks fervor and intensity. It is as if we
are living a skeletal life of the bare bones of faith.

[321]   **Eighth Rule.** The eighth: Let him who is in desolation labor to be in patience, which is contrary to the vexations which come to him: and let him think that he will soon be consoled, employing against the desolation the devices, as is said in the sixth Rule.

[322]   **Ninth Rule.** The ninth: There are three principal reasons why we find ourselves desolate.

The first is, because of our being tepid, lazy or negligent in our spiritual exercises; and so through our faults, spiritual consolation withdraws from us.

The second, to try us and see how much we are and how much we let ourselves out in His service and praise without such great pay of consolation and great graces.

The third, to give us true acquaintance and knowledge, that we may interiorly feel that it is not ours to get or keep great devotion, intense love, tears, or any other spiritual consolation, but that all is the gift and grace of God our Lord, and that we may not build a nest in a thing not ours, raising our intellect into some pride or vainglory, attributing to us devotion or the other things of the spiritual consolation.

[323]   **Tenth Rule.** The tenth: Let him who is in consolation think how he will be in the desolation which will come after, taking new strength for then.

[324]   **Eleventh Rule.** The eleventh: Let him who is consoled see to humbling himself and lowering himself as much as he can, thinking how little he is able for in the time of desolation without such grace or consolation.

On the contrary, let him who is in desolation think that he can do much with the grace sufficient to resist all his enemies, taking strength in his Creator and Lord.

[325]   **Twelfth Rule.** The twelfth: The enemy acts like a woman, in being weak against vigor and strong of will. Because, as it is the way of the woman when she is quarrelling with some man to lose heart, taking flight when the man shows her much courage: and on the contrary, if the man, losing heart, begins to fly, the wrath, revenge, and ferocity of the

8. The important attitude to nourish at a time of desolation is [321] patience. Patience can mitigate the frustration, dryness, or emptiness of the desolation period and so allow us to live through it a little less painfully. We should try to recall that everything has its time, and consolation has been ours in the past and will be God's gift in the future. Patience should mark even the efforts we undertake to work against the desolation which afflicts us.

9. Three important reasons why we suffer desolation are: [322]

(1) it is our own fault because we have not lived our life of faith with any effort. We have become tepid and slothful and our very shallowness in the spiritual life has brought about the experience of desolation;

(2) it is a trial period allowed by God. We find ourselves tested as to whether we love God or just love his gifts, whether we continue to follow his call in darkness and dryness as well as in light and consolation;

(3) it is a time when God lets us experience our own poverty and need. We see more clearly that the free gift of consolation is not something we can control, buy, or make our own.

> Next follow two guidelines dealing with spiritual
> consolation:

10. When we are enjoying a consolation period, we should use [323] foresight and savor the strength of such a period against the time when we may no longer find ourselves in consolation.

11. A time of consolation should provide the opportunity for [324] a growth in true humility. We can acknowledge with gratitude the gifts we have received and recognize the full gratuity of God's favor. It may be well to take stock how poorly we fare when such consolation is withdrawn.

On the other hand, if we are afflicted by desolation, we should take some consolation in knowing that God's grace is always sufficient to follow the way of the Lord.

> Through three images we can understand better
> the ways in which the evil spirit works.

12. The evil spirit often behaves like a spoiled child. If a [325] person is firm with such a child, the child gives up his petulant ways. But if a person shows indulgence or weakness in any way, the child is merciless in getting his own way by stomping his feet or by false displays of affection. So our tactics must include firmness in dealing with the evil spirit in our lives.

woman is very great, and so without bounds; in the same manner, it is the way of the enemy to weaken and lose heart, his temptations taking flight, when the person who is exercising himself in spiritual things opposes a bold front against the temptations of the enemy, doing diametrically the opposite. And on the contrary, if the person who is exercising himself commences to have fear and lose heart in suffering the temptations, there is no beast so wild on the face of the earth as the enemy of human nature in following out his damnable intention with so great malice.

[326]   **Thirteenth Rule.** The thirteenth: Likewise, he acts as a licentious lover in wanting to be secret and not revealed. For, as the licentious man who, speaking for an evil purpose, solicits a daughter of a good father or a wife of a good husband, wants his words and persuasions to be secret, and the contrary displeases him much, when the daughter reveals to her father or the wife to her husband his licentious words and depraved intention, because he easily gathers that he will not be able to succeed with the undertaking begun: in the same way, when the enemy of human nature brings his wiles and persuasions to the just soul, he wants and desires that they be received and kept in secret; but when one reveals them to his good Confessor or to another spiritual person that knows his deceits and evil ends, it is very grievous to him, because he gathers, from his manifest deceits being discovered, that he will not be able to succeed with his wickedness begun.

[327]   **Fourteenth Rule.** The fourteenth: Likewise, he behaves as a chief bent on conquering and robbing what he desires: for, as a captain and chief of the army, pitching his camp, and looking at the forces or defences of a stronghold, attacks it on the weakest side, in like manner the enemy of human nature, roaming about, looks in turn at all our virtues, theological, cardinal and moral; and where he finds us weakest and most in need for our eternal salvation, there he attacks us and aims at taking us.

13. The evil spirit's behavior can also be compared to a false [326] lover. The false lover uses other people for his own selfish ends, and so he uses people like objects at his disposal or as his playthings for entertainments and good times. He usually suggests that the so-called intimacy of the relationship be kept secret because he is afraid that his duplicity will become known. So the evil spirit often acts in order to keep his own suggestions and temptations secret, and our tactics must be to bring out into the light of day such suggestions and temptations to our confessor or director or superior.

14. The evil spirit can also work like a shrewd army com- [327] mander, who carefully maps out the tactics of attack at weak points of the defense. He knows that weakness is found in two ways: (a) the weakness of fragility or unpreparedness, and (b) the weakness of complacent strength which is pride. The evil spirit's attacks come against us at both of these points of weakness. The first kind of weakness is less serious in that we more readily acknowledge our need and cry out for help to the Lord. The second kind is far more serious and more devastating in its effect upon us so that it is a more favored tactic of the evil spirit.

[328]

RULES

FOR THE SAME EFFECT WITH

GREATER DISCERNMENT OF SPIRITS

AND THEY HELP MORE FOR THE SECOND WEEK

[329]   **First Rule.** The first: It is proper to God and to His Angels in their movements to give true spiritual gladness and joy, taking away all sadness and disturbance which the enemy brings on. Of this latter it is proper to fight against the spiritual gladness and consolation, bringing apparent reasons, subtleties and continual fallacies.

[330]   **Second Rule.** The second: It belongs to God our Lord to give consolation to the soul without preceding cause, for it is the property of the Creator to enter, go out and cause movements in the soul, bringing it all into love of His Divine Majesty. I say without cause: without any previous sense or knowledge of any object through which such consolation would come, through one's acts of understanding and will.

PART II. Guidelines Suitable Especially for the Second Week   [328]

The following statements are also meant to be helpful in understanding the interior movements which are a part of our spiritual lives. These guidelines are more subtle than the norms described in PART I because commonly in the progress of a good person's life the direction of all movements appears to be towards God and the proper development of one's spiritual life. These norms are especially helpful when a person experiences certain movements that commonly occur to persons engaged in the Second Week of the Exercises or thereafter.

A. A Statement of General Application

1. When we are trying to follow the call of the Lord in our   [329]
life, we will find that the good spirit tends to give support, encouragement, and oftentimes even a certain delight in all our endeavors.

The evil spirit generally acts to bring about the opposite reaction. The evil spirit will subtly arouse a dissatisfaction with our own efforts, will raise up doubts and anxieties about God's love or our own response, or sting the conscience with thoughts of pride in our attempt to lead a good life.

B. Particular Statements about Consolation

First, consolation is described in terms of its sources.
2. God alone can bring about consolation without any con-   [330]
comitant causes. We know the experience of having certain thoughts, achievements, or events which bring about a feeling of great consolation in our lives. We also know the effect of another person or persons whose very presence or conversation can give us joy. But we can more readily attribute our consolation directly to the touch of God when there is no thought, no event, no person—in general, no object of any sort—which seems to be the source of such a movement. The directness of sense words, such as "a touch" or "a taste," seems to point more accurately the way to describe this special action of God in our lives. The effect of such a taste or touch, which may bring along delight or joy, is what we can more readily grasp and speak about. But in these cases, we should be aware that God himself is truly said to be the direct source of all our consolation.

[331]   **Third Rule.** The third: With cause, as well the good Angel as the bad can console the soul, for contrary ends: the good Angel for the profit of the soul, that it may grow and rise from good to better, and the evil Angel, for the contrary, and later on to draw it to his damnable intention and wickedness.

[332]   **Fourth Rule.** The fourth: It is proper to the evil Angel, who forms himself under the appearance of an angel of light, to enter with the devout soul and go out with himself: that is to say, to bring good and holy thoughts, conformable to such just soul, and then little by little he aims at coming out drawing the soul to his covert deceits and perverse intentions.

[333]   **Fifth Rule.** The fifth: We ought to note well the course of the thoughts, and if the beginning, middle and end is all good, inclined to all good, it is a sign of the good Angel; but if in the course of the thoughts which he brings it ends in something bad, of a distracting tendency, or less good than what the soul had previously proposed to do, or if it weakens it or disquiets or disturbs the soul, taking away its peace, tranquillity and quiet, which it had before, it is a clear sign that it proceeds from the evil spirit, enemy of our profit and eternal salvation.

[334]   **Sixth Rule.** The sixth: When the enemy of human nature has been perceived and known by his serpent's tail and the bad end to which he leads on, it helps the person who was tempted by him, to look immediately at the course of the good thoughts which he brought him at their beginning, and how little by little he aimed at making him descend from the spiritual sweetness and joy in which he was, so far as to bring him to his depraved intention; in order that with this experience, known and noted, the person may be able to guard for the future against his usual deceits.

3. When there is a reason for consolation, whether it be from [331] certain thoughts or achievements or events, or even more so from certain people who have an effect upon us, then either the good spirit or the evil spirit can be involved. On the other hand, the good spirit brings about such consolation in order to strengthen and to speed the progress of our life in Christ. The evil spirit, on the other hand, arouses good feelings so that we are drawn to focus our attention on wrong things, or to pursue a more selfish motivation, or to find our own will before all else. Quietly and slowly the change is brought about until the evil direction becomes clear.

Ways of working with spurious consolation are:

4. For a person striving to lead a good life, the evil spirit [332] ordinarily begins like an angel of light. For example, we find ourselves inspired by pious thoughts or holy desires, and then after some time we are caught up in the pride of our own intellect and in the selfishness of our own desires.

5. We can become discerning persons by examining carefully [333] our own experiences. If in reflecting on the course of our thoughts or our actions we find that from beginning to end our eyes have remained fixed on the Lord, we can be sure that the good spirit has been moving us. But if what started off well in our thought and action begins to be self-focused or to turn us from our way to God, we should suspect that the evil spirit has somehow twisted the good beginning to an evil direction, and possibly even to an evil end. So we can discover that an original good course has led us to be weakened spiritually or even to become desolate or confused. The signs of desolation give clear indication of the evil spirit's influence.

6. When we recognize that we have been duped by the evil [334] spirit through a certain thought progression or course of action, we should review carefully all the stages which we passed through from the time when the evil became apparent back to its very beginnings in the good. By means of such a review, we will find that we can more quickly catch ourselves when we are being led on by the deceit of the evil spirit and so we are more enabled to guard ourselves in the future.

[335] **Seventh Rule.** The seventh: In those who go on from good to better, the good Angel touches such soul sweetly, lightly and gently, like a drop of water which enters into a sponge; and the evil touches it sharply and with noise and disquiet, as when the drop of water falls on the stone.

And the above-said spirits touch in a contrary way those who go on from bad to worse.

The reason of this is that the disposition of the soul is contrary or like to the said Angels. Because, when it is contrary, they enter perceptibly with clatter and noise; and when it is like, they enter with silence as into their own home, through the open door.

[336] **Eighth Rule.** The eighth: When the consolation is without cause, although there be no deceit in it, as being of God our Lord alone, as was said; still the spiritual person to whom God gives such consolation, ought, with much vigilance and attention, to look at and distinguish the time itself of such actual consolation from the following, in which the soul remains warm and favored with the favor and remnants of the consolation past; for often in this second time, through one's own course of habits and the consequences of the concepts and judgments, or through the good spirit or through the bad, he forms various resolutions and opinions which are not given immediately by God our Lord, and therefore they have need to be very well examined before entire credit is given them, or they are put into effect.

Finally, there are further insights in regard to consolation in the progress of our spiritual life:

7. As we continue to make progress in the spiritual life, the [335] movement of the good spirit is very delicate, gentle, and often delightful. It may be compared to the way a drop of water penetrates a sponge.

When the evil spirit tries to interrupt our progress, the movement is violent, disturbing, and confusing. It may be compared to the way a waterfall hits a stone ledge below.

In persons whose lives are going from bad to worse, the descriptions given above should just be reversed. The reason for this lies in the conflict of opposing forces. In other words, when good or evil spirits find our heart a true haven, they enter quietly just as anyone comes into his own home. By contrast, evil spirits cause great commotion and noise as they try to enter into the heart of the just person intent upon the good.

8. When the consolation experience in our life comes directly [336] from God, there can be no deception in it. Although a delight and a peace will be found in such an experience, a spiritual person should be very careful to distinguish the actual moment of this consolation-in-God-himself from the afterglow which may be exhilarating and joyful for some period of time. Quite often it is in this second period of time, that we begin to reason out plans of action or to make resolutions which cannot be attributed so directly to God as the initial experience which is non-conceptual in nature. Because human reasoning and other influences are now coming into the total picture of this consolation period, a very careful process of discerning the good and the evil spirits should be undertaken according to the previous guidelines before any resolution or plan of action is adopted.

[337]

IN THE MINISTRY OF
DISTRIBUTING ALMS

THE FOLLOWING RULES SHOULD BE KEPT

First Rule. The first: If I make the distribution to relatives or friends, or to persons for whom I have an affection, I shall have four things to see to, of which mention was made, in part, in the matter of Election.

The first is, that that love which moves me and makes me give the alms, should descend from above, from the love of God our Lord, so that I feel first in me that the love, more or less, which I have to such persons is for God; and that in the reason why I love them more, God appears.

[339]

Second Rule. The second: I want to set before me a man whom I have never seen or known, and desiring all his perfection in the ministry and condition which he has, as I would want him to keep the mean in his manner of distributing, for the greater glory of God our Lord and the greater perfection of his soul; I, doing so, neither more nor less, will keep the rule and measure which I should want and judge to be right for the other.

GUIDELINES FOR THE CHRISTIAN SHARING [337]

OF ONE'S WEALTH AND POSSESSIONS

Preliminary Note: St. Ignatius of Loyola wrote these guidelines as a help for a special group of retreatants who played a most important part in the Christian society of his day. These people had certain responsibilities to the poor and needy because of ecclesiastical benefices or specified inheritances. They faced special obligations in the area of Christian charity because of their office or ministry.

Even though the particular ministry of distributing alms was the historical stimulus to Ignatius' guidelines, we can still find helpful the attitudes which he proposes for our own Christian sharing with those in need today.

In our Christian sharing of our own wealth and resources, the following guidelines are meant to be helpful:

1. Our first concern should be about ourselves and the way [344] we live. We should try to live modestly by simplifying our lifestyle as much as possible and by becoming more aware of being thrifty in our use of our world's resources. We should try to image in our lives the attitudes and way of living which we see in Jesus Christ, our model, guide, and Lord.

Historically we have the example of the Third Church Council of Carthage, at which St. Augustine was present. This Council made the decree that the bishop, after the manner of Christ our High Priest, should make himself a model of true Christian living, by observing a simple life-style, especially in terms of his possessions.

In a similar way, all Christian men and women should adapt this kind of simplicity in their life style, according to their office and position in the society in which they live.

By a pious tradition, we have the example of Mary's parents, St. Joachim and St. Anne. They divided what they possessed in

[340]   **Third Rule.** The third: I want to consider, as if I were at the point of death, the form and measure which then I should want to have kept in the office of my administration, and regulating myself by that, to keep it in the acts of my distribution.

[341]   **Fourth Rule.** The fourth: Looking how I shall find myself on the Day of Judgment, to think well how then I should want to have used this office and charge of administration; and the rule which then I should want to have kept, to keep it now.

three ways. The first part they gave to the poor. The second they divided for the upkeep and services of the Temple. And the third they used for their own support.

When I consider sharing what I have with those to whom I have some natural obligations, such as family relations, friends, or those persons who hold a certain place in my heart, there are certain criteria to be followed. Some of these were mentioned when we considered the Choice of a State or Way of Life (see [169] above). [338]

1. The love that moves me to want to share with these people for whom I have an affection should be grounded in my love of God our Lord. It is the love of God that moves and stimulates me to express my care and affection in the very sharing of what I have. I should be aware that deeper down than the stimulus which comes from my natural feeling and concern I am moved by God, and he is the source for my being able to love these people ever more fully.

2. In order to maintain better a certain objectivity in regard to the people for whom I feel affection and with whom I want to share what I have, I place myself in an imaginary relationship with a person whom I have never seen or known. He has a certain responsibility to share what he has, and I want him to be able to do this as well as he can according to his way of life. When I consider the measure of sharing which this person does because he is moved by his love of the Lord, I discover a proper mean for myself and I should act on it. As a result, according to the standard which I rejoice in seeing this person observe, I find my own rule of action. [339]

3. Another help in reaching objectivity in regard to the people for whom I feel affection and with whom I want to share what I have is found in the consideration of my own death. If I picture myself at the hour of my death, I can ponder what norm I would like to have observed in fulfilling my responsibilities of Christian charity. This norm I will take upon myself now and observe it in my attempts to share the goods which I call my own. [340]

4. Another help can be the consideration of my own personal judgment before the Lord on the day of my death. I can well imagine what account I would like to give to the Lord in the area of carrying out my Christian responsibilities of charity. [341]

[342]   **Fifth Rule.** The fifth: When some person feels himself inclined and drawn to some persons to whom he wants to distribute alms, let him hold himself back and ponder well the above-mentioned four Rules, examining and testing his affection by them; and not give the alms until, conformably to them, he has in all dismissed and cast out his disordered inclination.

[343]   **Sixth Rule.** The sixth: Although there is no fault in taking the goods of God our Lord to distribute them, when the person is called by God our Lord to such ministry; still in the quantity of what he has to take and apply to himself out of what he has to give to others, there may be doubt as to fault and excess. Therefore, he can reform in his life and condition by the above-mentioned Rules.

[344]   **Seventh Rule.** The seventh: For the reasons already mentioned and for many others, it is always better and more secure in what touches one's person and condition of life to spare more and diminish and approach more to our High Priest, our model and rule, who is Christ our Lord; conformably to what the third Council of Carthage, in which St. Augustine was, determines and orders — that the furniture of the Bishop be cheap and poor. The same should be considered in all manners of life, looking at and deciding according to the condition and state of the persons; as in married life we have the example of St. Joachim and of St. Ann, who, dividing their means into three parts, gave the first to the poor, and the second to the ministry and service of the Temple, and took the third for the support of themselves and of their household.

The same way of acting which I would want to be true on judgment day I can now begin to observe and live out.

The preceding four criteria are meant to help me when I feel [342] moved to share what I have because of the natural inclinations and affection which I find within myself. I should test my freedom from all disordered attachments by these criteria. I should not begin to share my goods until I can feel myself free to act, no longer under the influence of any disordered attachment.

When it is a matter of my own job or position bringing me [343] into the responsibility of distributing money or goods, I may find that God truly calls me to this way of life. The danger may lie in the manner in which I execute this job or office—using the funds and resources to my own enhancement, comfort, and privilege. I should look to the criteria already given in order that I might better fulfill my God-given responsibility.

[345]

THE FOLLOWING NOTES HELP TO PERCEIVE
AND UNDERSTAND

SCRUPLES

AND PERSUASIONS OF OUR ENEMY

[346]   **First Note.** The first: They commonly call a scruple what proceeds from our own judgment and freedom: that is to say, when I freely decide that that is sin which is not sin, as when it happens that after some one has accidentally stepped on a cross of straw, he decides with his own judgment that he has sinned.

This is properly an erroneous judgment and not a real scruple.

[347]   **Second Note.** The second: After I have stepped on that cross, or after I have thought or said or done some other thing, there comes to me a thought from without that I have sinned, and on the other hand it appears to me that I have not sinned; still I feel disturbance in this; that is to say, in as much as I doubt and in as much as I do not doubt.

That is a real scruple and temptation which the enemy sets.

[348]   **Third Note.** Third: The first scruple — of the first note — is much to be abhorred, because it is all error; but the second — of the second note — for some space of time is of no little profit to the soul which is giving itself to spiritual exercises;[1] rather in great manner it purifies and cleanses such a soul, separating it much from all appearance of sin: according to that saying of Gregory: "It belongs to good minds to see a fault where there is no fault."

[349]   **Fourth Note.** The fourth: The enemy looks much if a soul is gross or delicate, and if

---

[1] Exercises *is added by St. Ignatius.*

SOME NOTES CONCERNING SCRUPLES [345-

St. Ignatius of Loyola was troubled severely by scruples in the early Manresan days (1522-1523) of his conversion. His notes about scruples undoubtedly come from his own experience as well as from his attempt to help others. In the light of modern psychology and pastoral counseling, there is a certain naiveté present in these notes. Perhaps Ignatius' own nondescript title of "Notes" indicates the less than definitive nature of these reflections. Although some help can still be derived from these notes, there seemed to be less purpose in rendering them in a more contemporary style. Instead, the following observations are made, along with some further reading references.

1. The traditional approach to scrupulosity, represented soundly enough in St. Ignatius' Notes, was quick to identify the problem as a direct trial inflicted by the devil or a special probing by God for his own spiritual purposes. Today with the help provided by modern psychology and psychiatry, most experienced spiritual directors would agree that there is a greater complexity in clarifying the experience of scrupulosity.

2. Until very recently confessors were often encouraged to become the conscience for the person who is afflicted by scruples. Presently scruples are not seen so exclusively as an ailment of our conscience. For in many cases when we are suffering from scruples, we know what is objectively right or wrong and so our conscience is functioning quite well. The real problem in this instance lies more in the emotional area which paralyzes us and prevents us from applying our correct conclusions to ourselves with any degree of comfort.

3. Commonly, scruples are rooted in the emotion of fear—a general anxiety about leading the good life or a fixed anxiety about one area of life such as the sexual. Scruples arising from a neurotic compulsion also take on varying forms in people—compulsion over the letter of the law in general or compulsion in regard to one small area of legal perfection.

4. Scrupulosity, rooted as it is more within our emotions than in our judgment, needs the help of a person experienced in counseling. With such help we can begin to uncover the roots of our emotional disturbance and so start to work with and integrate these experiences of scrupulosity. If the case of scruples

it is delicate, he tries to make it more delicate in the extreme, to disturb and embarrass it more. For instance, if he sees that a soul does not consent to either mortal sin or venial or any appearance of deliberate sin, then the enemy, when he cannot make it fall into a thing that appears sin, aims at making it make out sin where there is not sin, as in a word or very small thought.

If the soul is gross, the enemy tries to make it more gross; for instance, if before it made no account of venial sins, he will try to have it make little account of mortal sins, and if before it made some account, he will try to have it now make much less or none.

[350]   **Fifth Note.** The fifth: The soul which desires to benefit itself in the spiritual life, ought always to proceed the contrary way to what the enemy proceeds; that is to say, if the enemy wants to make the soul gross, let it aim at making itself delicate. Likewise, if the enemy tries to draw it out to extreme fineness, let the soul try to establish itself in the mean, in order to quiet itself in everything.

[351]   **Sixth Note.** The sixth: When such good soul wants to speak or do something within the Church, within the understanding of our Superiors, and which should be for the glory of God our Lord, and there comes to him a thought or temptation from without that he should neither say nor do that thing — bringing to him apparent reasons of vainglory or of another thing, etc., — then he ought to raise his understanding to his Creator and Lord, and if he sees that it is His due service, or at the least not contrary to it, he ought to act diametrically against such temptation, according to St. Bernard, answering the same: "Neither for thee did I begin, nor for thee will I stop."

is acute, the aid of a psychologist or psychiatrist is recommended.

5. Spiritual literature makes us aware of another phenomenon. In the development of our spiritual life, there can be a true awakening of conscience to a wholly new delicacy of conscience. If we have been living at a certain superficial level of security or certainty about the quality of our Christian faith, we are shaken out of that complacency by some kind of strong religious experience.

Properly speaking, the temporary lack of certitude and firmness of judgment aroused by this experience is not scrupulosity. Instead, this is recognized traditionally as a symptom of growth —a period of time when we need careful guidance to grow in our response to God's call. We desire to move beyond the now-recognized dullness or obtuseness of our conscience because we are roused by a new sensitivity of love.

6. Both in the case of scruples properly so called and in the case of a person being awakened to a true God-given delicacy of conscience, the support, patience, and encouragement of a confessor or spiritual director is most helpful.

7. The experience of scrupulosity in our life can be integrated like any other apparently harmful or personally diminishing experience. Insofar as it is integrated, we further our spiritual growth and maturity, and we also come to a new delicacy of conscience.

Further References
Bernard Häring, C.Ss.R., *Shalom: Peace. The Sacrament of Reconciliation* (New York: Farrer, Straus, and Giroux, 1967), pp. 294-299.
Norman Camerson, Ph.D., *Personality Development and Psychopathology* (Boston: Houghton Mifflin Company, 1963), pp. 373-411.

[352]

TO HAVE THE TRUE SENTIMENT

WHICH WE OUGHT TO HAVE IN THE CHURCH
MILITANT

Let the following Rules be observed.

[353]   **First Rule.** The first: All judgment laid aside, we ought to have our mind ready and prompt to obey, in all, the true Spouse of Christ our Lord, which is our holy Mother the Church Hierarchical.

[354]   **Second Rule.** The second: To praise confession to a Priest, and the reception of the most Holy Sacrament of the Altar once in the year, and much more each month, and much better from week to week, with the conditions required and due.

[355]   **Third Rule.** The third: To praise the hearing of Mass often, likewise [1] hymns, psalms, and long prayers, in the church and out of it; likewise the hours set at the time fixed for each Divine Office and for all prayer and all Canonical Hours.

[356]   **Fourth Rule.** The fourth: To praise much Religious Orders, virginity and continence, and not so much marriage as any of these.

---

[1] Likewise *is added in St. Ignatius' hand.*

GUIDELINES ON THINKING WITH THE CHURCH TODAY [352]

Preliminary Note. St. Ignatius of Loyola was convinced that the man or woman who makes the thirty day Exercises would be taking on a more active and concerned role in the life of the Church. In the midst of the confusion and turmoil of the sixteenth-century Church of his day, he knew the difficulty of maintaining a mature balance, a clear-headed judgment, and a loving reverence for both tradition and change. The guidelines which he proposed were meant to be internalized by the retreatant, just as the Guidelines with regard to Eating or the Guidelines for the Discernment of Spirits. In this way, a person could come more easily to responsible judgment and action in everyday life. Even though Ignatius' statements were made in the light of events in the Church of his day, the elements which he includes in his reflections have a lasting value for our own behavior.

The following statements are meant to be helpful in developing a true and loving sensitivity to the ways of thinking, feeling, and acting as a Catholic in our present-day Church.

1. When legitimate authority speaks within the Church, we [353] should listen with receptive ears and be more prompt to respond favorably than to criticize in a condemnatory way.

2. We should praise and reverence the sacramental life in the [354] Church, especially encouraging a more personal involvement and a more frequent participation in the celebration of the Eucharist and of the sacrament of reconciliation.

3. We should praise and reverence the prayer life in the [355] Church, especially as it has been developed in the Eucharistic celebration and in the public morning and evening praise service of the Divine Office.

4. We should praise and esteem all vocations as God-given [356] within the Church—married life, the dedicated single life, the priestly life, and the religious life.

[357]   **Fifth Rule.** The fifth: To praise vows of Religion, of obedience, of poverty, of chastity and of other perfections of supererogation. And it is to be noted that as the vow is about the things which approach to Evangelical perfection, a vow ought not to be made in the things which withdraw from it, such as to be a merchant, or to be married, etc.

[358]   **Sixth Rule.** To praise relics of the Saints, giving veneration to them and praying to the Saints; and to praise Stations, pilgrimages, Indulgences, pardons, Cruzadas, and candles lighted in the churches.

[359]   **Seventh Rule.** To praise Constitutions about fasts and abstinence, as of Lent, Ember Days, Vigils, Friday and Saturday; likewise penances, not only interior, but also exterior.

[360]   **Eighth Rule.** To praise the ornaments and the buildings of churches; likewise images, and to venerate them according to what they represent.

[361]   **Ninth Rule.** Finally, to praise all precepts of the Church, keeping the mind prompt to find reasons in their defence and in no manner against them.

[362]   **Tenth Rule.** We ought to be more prompt to find good and praise as well the Constitutions and recommendations as the ways of our Superiors. Because, although some are not or have not been such, to speak against them, whether preaching in public or discoursing before the common people, would rather give rise to fault-finding and scandal than profit; and so the people would be incensed against their Superiors, whether temporal or spiritual. So that, as it does harm to speak evil to the common people of Superiors in their absence, so it can make profit to speak of the evil ways to the persons themselves who can remedy them.

[363]   **Eleventh Rule.** To praise positive and scholastic learning. Because, as it is more proper to the Positive Doctors, as St. Jerome,

5. We should praise the religiously vowed life of poverty, [357] chastity, and obedience as the special sign of God's call to a Kingdom whose value system stands in contrast to the value system of our world.

6. We should have a loving reverence for all the men and [358] women who have gone before us and make up the communion of saints, especially those whom the Church has identified as helpers for us in our own struggling lives here and now. Our prayers for their support and our various devotions are our living out of the mystery that we all form the one communion of saints and that there is a continuing concern of all the members for one another.

7. We should respect the Christian call to penance and should [359] respond freely to the abstinence and fasting of the prescribed days in the Church year. We should also continue our personal search for ways of giving expression to the carrying of our cross daily in our following of Jesus Christ.

8. We should show respect for our places of worship and for [360] the statues, paintings, and decorations which are an attempt to beautify them and help us in praising God.

9. The law and precepts within the Church are meant to be of [361] help for the institutional life of the Body of Christ. As a result, we should maintain a proper respect for such laws and respond full-heartedly to them for the good order of the whole Body.

10. We should be more ready to give our support and appro- [362] val to our leaders, both in their personal conduct and in their directives, than to find fault with them. Only greater dissatis- faction and disunity among us is caused by public criticism and defamation of character. Rather the proper steps in remedying a wrong, harmful, unjust, or scandalous situation would be to refer and make representation to the persons who can do some- thing about the problem.

11. We should praise and respect the work of the theologians [363] in our Church, especially those who have given us the legacy of positive and scholastic doctrine. Some men, such as St. Jerome, St. Augustine, and St. Gregory, have given us their theological reflections in a way that we are moved to a greater love and service of God. Today, too, some theologians write in

St. Augustine and St. Gregory, etc., to move the heart to love and serve God our Lord in everything; so it is more proper to the Scholastics, as St. Thomas, St. Bonaventure, and to the Master of the Sentences, etc., to define or explain for our times [1] the things necessary for eternal salvation; and to combat and explain better all errors and all fallacies. For the Scholastic Doctors, as they are more modern, not only help themselves with the true understanding of the Sacred Scripture and of the Positive and holy Doctors, but also, they being enlightened and clarified by the Divine virtue, help themselves by the Councils, Canons and Constitutions of our holy Mother the Church.

[364]   **Twelfth Rule.** We ought to be on our guard in making comparison of those of us who are alive to the blessed passed away, because error is committed not a little in this; that is to say, in saying, this one knows more than St. Augustine; he is another, or greater than, St. Francis; he is another St. Paul in goodness, holiness, etc.

[365]   **Thirteenth Rule.** To be right in everything, we ought always to hold that the white which I see, is black, if the Hierarchical Church so decides it, believing that between Christ our Lord, the Bridegroom, and the Church, His Bride, there is the same Spirit which governs and directs us for the salvation of our souls. Because by the same Spirit and our Lord Who gave the ten Commandments, our holy Mother the Church is directed and governed.

[366]   **Fourteenth Rule.** Although there is much truth in the assertion that no one can save himself without being predestined and without having faith and grace; we must be very cautious in the manner of speaking and communicating with others about all these things.

---

[1] Or explain for our times *is added in the Saint's handwriting.*

this more devotional way. Others, such as St. Thomas Aquinas, St. Bonaventure, and Peter Lombard (the Master of the Sentences), define and explain doctrine in order to clarify Christian mysteries through analogies and to expose error and fallacious thinking. Some theologians today continue this process, and their writings are often more difficult and less appealing than the first group mentioned. But both kinds of theologians are important for the reflective life of the Church. The modern theologians have this advantage: Moved and enlightened by the grace of God, they have not only the legacy of the men before them and the rich development of Scripture studies, but also very importantly the whole tradition of the official Church's teaching as summed up in Church Councils, decrees, and constitutions up to the present time.

12. We sometimes act as if we have discovered Christianity [364] and true holiness for the first time in our own day. And so we have the tendency to exaggerate the contribution of a particular person in our contemporary Church or the holiness of life exemplified in certain practices. We should avoid making comparisons which attempt to exalt some of our own present-day leaders and practices at the expense of past peoples and traditions.

13. We believe that Christ our Lord has shared his Spirit with [365] the Church in a lasting way. The Spirit, then, is present in the whole Church and its leaders, and continues the influence and guidance which her leadership gives to all the faithful. Although there may be matters which we as individuals at times cannot see or grasp, the Church may have given some direction about it in order to aid us in our Christian life. In the area of the infallibility of the dogmas defined by the Church, we must surrender our own private judgment. We should be more open to acknowledge the limitations of our own individual opinion than to scorn the light of the Spirit's action within the tradition and communal vision of a Church which is described as truly catholic.

14. It will always remain difficult to describe adequately the [366] saving will of God. That God wants all men to be saved is revealed. That man has the freedom to reject God in a decisive way is also our belief. We should be careful in our thinking and speaking about this matter not to begin to deny either of these two essential statements of our Christian faith.

[367]   **Fifteenth Rule.** We ought not, by way of custom, to speak much of predestination; but if in some way and at some times one speaks, let him so speak that the common people may not come into any error, as sometimes happens, saying: Whether I have to be saved or condemned is already determined, and no other thing can now be, through my doing well or ill; and with this, growing lazy, they become negligent in the works which lead to the salvation and the spiritual [1] profit of their souls.

[368]   **Sixteenth Rule.** In the same way, we must be on our guard that by talking much and with much insistence of faith, without any distinction and explanation, occasion be not given to the people to be lazy and slothful in works, whether before faith is formed in charity or after.

[369]   **Seventeenth Rule.** Likewise, we ought not to speak so much with insistence on grace that the poison of discarding liberty be engendered.

So that of faith and grace one can speak as much as is possible with the Divine help for the greater praise of His Divine Majesty, but not in such way, nor in such manners, especially in our so dangerous times, that works and free will receive any harm, or be held for nothing.

[370]   **Eighteenth Rule.** Although serving God our Lord much out of pure love is to be esteemed above all; we ought to praise much the fear of His Divine Majesty, because not only filial fear is a thing pious and most holy, but even servile fear — when the man reaches nothing else better or more useful — helps much to get out of mortal sin. And when he is out, he easily comes to filial fear, which is all acceptable and grateful to God our Lord, as being at one with the Divine Love.

---

[1] Spiritual *is added in St. Ignatius' handwriting.*

15. Because we must work out our salvation through our whole [367] lifetime by the grace of God, we must avoid the two following extremes. Being pessimistic to the point of despair, we could act as if we have no ability to act freely or to change and so we deny the God-given gift of our personal freedom as well as the power of his grace, with which we must cooperate. Or being presumptuous, we could act as if we ourselves can change and grow and become perfect solely through our own efforts, with God and his grace being incidental to our salvation.

16. From what has been said above, there is always the danger [368] of so stressing the importance of faith in God and his grace for our salvation that we ignore the necessity of living out lives of active love for our neighbor and for our world.

17. Similarly, we can so stress the power of grace that we can [369] be remiss in taking the human means to remedy physical, psychological, and spiritual evils. We must not try to escape from the responsibility to use our freedom and to choose from all the various means for our growth and development which God has given us in our contemporary world.

18. Today we have a great emphasis on the motivation of love [370] being central to our Christian lives. Yet we can so overstress a language of love, that we ignore the value of Christian fear—the fear of the Lord which acknowledges God as God and the filial fear of offending a Father who loves us. And so in the practical living of our Christian lives, we must acknowledge and make use of the various motivating factors which lead us on in our growth and development.

GENERAL INDEX